513.2
W/

Charles Sturt University
Library

1196052

Numeracy and
Learning Difficulties

Approaches to teaching and assessment

Peter Westwood

To my very dear friend Lam Ching Wah (Vivian)
An exemplary teacher and a true professional

Numeracy and
Learning Difficulties

Approaches to teaching and assessment

Peter Westwood

Charles Sturt University
Library

First published 2000
by The Australian Council for Educational Research Ltd
19 Prospect Hill Road, Camberwell, Victoria, 3124

10 9 8 7 6 5 4 3 2

Copyright © 2000 Peter Westwood

All rights reserved. Except under the conditions described in the
Copyright Act 1968 of Australia and subsequent amendments,
no part of this publication may be reproduced, stored in a
retrieval system or transmitted in any form or by any means,
electronic, mechanical, photocopying, recording or otherwise,
without the written permission of the publishers.

Edited by Adrienne de Kretser
Designed and typeset by Polar Design Pty Ltd
Cover designed by Polar Design Pty Ltd
Printed by McPhersons Printing Group

National Library of Australia Cataloguing-in-Publication data:

Westwood, Peter S. (Peter Stuart), 1936–.
Numeracy and learning difficulties : approaches to teaching
and assessment.

Bibliography.
Includes index.
ISBN 0 86431 341 1.

1. Numeracy – Study and teaching (Primary). 2. Number
concept in children. I. Australian Council for Educational
Research. II. Title.

372.72044

Contents

Preface

Until fairly recent times the term 'numeracy' was usually taken simply to mean adequate competence in applying the basic skills of arithmetic necessary for coping with everyday situations. More recently, although retaining the same 'everyday functional use' connotation, the concept of numeracy has been expanded considerably. Numeracy isn't just possessing some mechanical facility with numbers: it also embraces the notion of being able to communicate effectively with others through the basic language of mathematics, to interpret everyday quantitative information, and to have a repertoire of strategies and 'number sense' to deal with problems that may arise (Willis 1998). Numeracy includes not only an understanding of and competence with basic number and measurement, but also skills and confidence in the handling and interpretation of quantitative data (Peach 1998). Steen (1997, p. xvii) describes numeracy as 'quantitative literacy', and by doing so implies that it is as important for an individual to be numerate in today's world as it is to be able to read and write proficiently.

In Australia, as in other countries, the development of numeracy skills is being given high priority in the school curriculum. Ellison (1998, p. 27) states that, 'A high standard of numeracy is vital if our young people are to operate effectively in a complex technological society and realise their goals and potential'. It is an unfortunate fact, however, that too many of our students experience difficulty in learning basic mathematics. For them, a satisfactory level of numeracy is an unattained goal.

This is not a book about identifying students with learning difficulties in basic mathematics and removing them from class for intensive 'remediation' (although such intervention will be necessary for a few students). It is a book that argues for high-quality 'first teaching' to prevent students failing in the initial acquisition of numeracy skills. While many of the teaching and assessment strategies described are equally applicable to small group work and to individual tuition, the aim is actually to explore and encourage more effective classroom teaching. The argument put forward is that the most effective approach is one that combines important and successful aspects of direct teaching with the most meaningful and motivating components of student-centred, constructivist approaches.

It is true that in the past, at all age levels, mathematics was taught through predominantly didactic methods, with too much emphasis placed on rote memorisation of rules and 'tricks' to obtain the 'right' answers. The students' learning was much too procedural rather than conceptual, hence the call for a reform in the teaching of mathematics. The widely advocated solution is for a shift toward constructivist, student-centred, enquiry-based approaches, in the belief that students understand best the knowledge they acquire through their own activity and exploration. These constructivist approaches are being advocated so strongly that there is a real danger that the educational pendulum will swing so far in the opposite direction that teachers will feel that they must abandon all forms of direct teaching. The argument presented in *Numeracy and Learning Difficulties* is that, for effective acquisition of numeracy skills, a balanced approach is required, combining the best of the new knowledge about students' learning with the best of traditional pedagogy.

PETER WESTWOOD
UNIVERSITY OF HONG KONG

1 Developing numeracy: current issues in learning and teaching

The difficulties and frustrations of mathematics teaching in schools are widely recognised. Far too many of our young children find learning mathematics in school difficult, lose their confidence in mathematics, and go on to join that large swathe of the adult population who panic at the first sight of numbers (Whitebread 1995, p.11).

In the domain of numeracy education, three main issues of concern have emerged in recent years. The first is the recognition that too many students do not enjoy mathematics as a subject and do not experience success in this area of the school curriculum. The second is a new perspective on how children acquire mathematical skills and concepts, together with new theories on how best to teach them. The third is the evidence from cross-cultural research studies such as the Third International Mathematics and Science Study (TIMSS) that mathematics achievement in some countries is vastly superior to achievement in other countries, thus increasing interest in the impact of cultural influences and different teaching methods. This chapter addresses each of these issues, to provide a foundation for the chapters that follow.

'I hate maths!'

On the issue of student disenchantment with the subject, Wain (1994) considers it very sad that mathematics teaching over the years has failed so many students by not providing them with stimulation, understanding, enjoyment and a feeling of success. He points out that many intelligent people, after an average of 1500 hours of instruction over eleven years of schooling, still regard mathematics as a meaningless activity for which they have no aptitude. He concludes that, 'it is difficult to imagine how a subject could have achieved for itself such an appaling image as it now has in the popular mind … to think that all our effort has led to a situation of fear and loathing is depressing' (p. 31).

Not only do some students dislike school mathematics and lose confidence in their own abilities (Burton 1994a), a few develop an almost pathological dread of the subject. Their negativity is so strong that they become extremely stressed and anxious in any situation involving the use of numbers. 'Maths anxiety', 'maths panic' and 'maths phobia' have become popular topics for educational research (e.g. Buxton 1991). Based on my own experience tutoring students with chronic learning failure in mathematics, it appears to be true that many of them require personal counselling and emotional support in addition to skilled teaching.

McCoy (1995) suggests that students with learning difficulties seem to regard mathematics as a 'cold, indifferent' body of knowledge, far removed from everyday life and of no immediate practical value. Their antipathy toward the subject continues into adult life, as reflected in this comment from the *National statement on mathematics for Australian schools*: 'There is considerable anecdotal and research evidence to suggest that many people dislike mathematics and may even feel intimidated in situations in which it is used' (Australian Education Council 1994, p. 7). This echoes a similar comment in a much earlier study in Britain, where it was reported that for a significant number of adults 'the need to undertake even an apparently simple and straightforward piece of mathematics could induce feelings of anxiety, helplessness, fear and even guilt' (Department of Education and Science 1982, p. 7).

Among the many negative things people say to themselves about mathematics, the following are fairly typical: 'Maths really worries me and makes me anxious'; 'Maths is no fun'; 'It's hard and boring' (Costello, Horne & Munro 1992). They also suggest that failures are due to their own lack of ability rather than to poor teaching: 'I'm too stupid to do it'; 'I just can't deal with numbers'. This external locus of control contributes to their learned helplessness and negative expectations in relation to mathematics. As people get older, their difficulties often intensify and their confidence and motivation become seriously eroded (Salend 1994).

We need to ask why this situation exists. Why do so many students and adults hate mathematics? Is the subject matter so complex that only a few fortunate students with an innate aptitude for dealing with numbers can ever hope to make sense of it? Does a high proportion of the population suffer from 'dyscalculia' — a specific learning disability equivalent to dyslexia in the literacy domain? Or is the quality of mathematics teaching in schools at fault? Can the high failure rate be attributed in any way to poor or inappropriate instruction? We will return to these questions in a moment.

It is important to state from the beginning that, within the large population of students who have difficulties in acquiring numeracy skills, there is no convincing evidence (with a few exceptions) that their problems result from any lack of innate potential or from cognitive deficits. They are not deficient in some essential part of their intellect that deals with quantitative experience, making it impossible for them to deal with number relationships and other mathematical concepts. Of course, in a few cases there are underlying reasons that help to account for learning problems (Clayton 1999), and in a moment we will look briefly at these causes. It would be quite wrong, however, to give the impression that these psychological and perceptual factors are primary causes in most cases of failure.

Such an assumption creates a situation where the solution to students' numeracy problems is believed to be the provision of more specialist remedial tuition, rather than an improvement in the way numeracy skills are taught to all students.

Why do students fail?

There are probably many reasons for students' failure in mathematics, and most of them are likely to be based within the curriculum and the teaching method, rather than within the learner (Vaughn, Bos & Schumm 1997). This important issue of pedagogical causes will be discussed fully in this and other chapters. First, however, it is necessary to consider briefly some of the less common 'within the learner' characteristics that can cause or exacerbate learning problems for a few students.

In the learning disabilities field, for many years the focus was almost entirely upon language, reading and writing skills: relatively little attention was given to students' learning problems in mathematics. Recently, however, much more attention has been paid to mathematics (e.g. Chinn & Ashcroft 1998; Grauberg 1998; Miles & Miles 1992; Stewart 1997). Some of these writers appear to subscribe to the 'deficit model' of learning difficulties, attributing learning problems to weaknesses in students' underlying cognitive processes. Grauberg (1998), for example, discusses weaknesses in symbolic understanding, weaknesses in organisational skills, memory problems, difficulties with auditory discrimination, and so on. Others (e.g. McCoy 1995) describe poor concentration span, poor motivation, inefficient learning style, passivity, negativity, anxiety and task avoidance. One must wonder whether these so-called deficits are more a reflection of the teaching approach used and the curriculum being taught, than the predisposition of the learner. Although these factors may contribute to problems in school learning, teachers should not regard them as barriers that will always prevent a student from making progress. Careful programming and skilled teaching can reduce the impact of these negative factors. For every item in the deficit list above there is a direct implication for modifying or adapting instruction, not an excuse for failing to teach. As Ginsburg (1989, p. 237) has remarked, 'The most effective strategy for dealing with learning problems is to improve the quality of instruction'.

Recent criticisms of mathematics teaching

Even allowing for individual differences in aptitude for mathematics learning, and possible weaknesses in cognitive processing in a few cases, much of the problem of learning failure appears to stem from the quality of teaching. Kamii (1994), Pound (1999) and Whitebread (1995) are only three among many mathematics educators who suggest that the cause of children's turning away from mathematics lies in the way that mathematics is taught. They suggest that the teaching, even in the early years of schooling, is too far removed from children's everyday experiences. It is argued that in many classrooms 'mathematics' is still restricted to teaching arithmetic procedures, with little attention given to developing conceptual understanding and problem-solving strategies. As Booker et al. (1997, p. 8) comment, 'If the mathematics to be introduced cannot be related to the child's experiences, it simply will not make sense and the child will be reduced to manipulating meaningless symbols using rules that are not understood'.

A cat ate 2 fish for breakfast, 3 fish for lunch and 5 fish for tea. How many fish did the cat eat altogether?

Kamii (1994) and Meadows (1993) indicate that teaching formal number skills to young children too early can be the beginning of their experience of failure. Students do not understand how classroom number work relates to the real world. They lose the intuitive sense of number relationships that was developing very soundly, by informal means, before they came to school. Whitebread (1995, p. 15), for example, describes the case of a seven-year-old girl who gave up using a perfectly acceptable informal strategy for subtraction because it did not seem to be the way that her teacher wanted subtraction to be done. When asked at a common-sense level what her answer to a school arithmetic problem actually meant, she replied, 'Nothing, silly, it's a sum'.

Another criticism of mathematics teaching is that traditionally it has been based on a 'transmission' model of instruction. The teacher is seen as the knowledgeable expert who will transfer to the minds of learners, by direct instruction, what he or she knows. The transmission model of teaching assumes that learners will absorb ideas and make meaning from the information and explanations provided by the teacher. Learners will also acquire specific skills by observing and imitating the demonstrations and actions of the teacher. This model gives the teacher the active role (as presenter) and learners the passive role, ready to receive knowledge and skills. Stigler, Fernandez and Yoshida (1996, p. 150) argue against this model of teaching and learning. They state that, 'The student is not an empty vessel into which knowledge must be loaded but an active participant in the process of knowledge construction (and) learning mathematics results from students' own thinking, not from training them in specific processes'.

Reforming the teaching of mathematics

The most recent cry is for teaching methods to be driven by what we know about children's learning. It is argued that children learn best when they participate in activities that are relevant to them, hold their attention and require them to 'make meaning' for themselves. This approach is based on the theory of learning known as 'constructivism'. Richards (1996, p. 71) sums up this perspective: 'In the process of teaching we need to understand that each individual must, ultimately, construct his or her own mathematics'. It is argued that, to facilitate the process, enquiry-based and active learning methods in 'resource-rich environments' are required (Burton 1994b).

Current recommendations for reform in mathematics teaching are based on this notion of constructive learning, and call for greatly increased emphasis on meaningful experiences and decreased emphasis on the repeated drilling of decontextualised arithmetic procedures (Manouchehri & Goodman 1998; Simon 1997). Wakefield (1997) makes the point that teaching methods that stress rote memorisation of basic number facts and algorithmic procedures are usually boring and do not require learners to participate actively in thought and reflection.

According to Borasi (1996), successful functioning in today's world requires students to become problem-solvers and critical thinkers, rather than merely proficient in the computational processes of arithmetic. To achieve this outcome, Boaler (1997) argues that approaches to mathematics must become more 'authentic' and less 'algorithmic', with emphasis on student-centred and project-based problem-solving. Such an approach is more likely to produce knowledge that is adaptable to new contexts and can be used in the real world.

Constructivism: the dominant theory

In recent years, teachers in Australia have been very actively persuaded to use constructivist approaches in most curriculum areas, particularly in domains such as language arts, mathematics, science, technology and environmental education. In a small study of teachers in South Australia, 79% of younger respondents reported that in their initial teacher-training courses and during in-service programs, they had been strongly advised to use a constructivist approach in mathematics teaching (Westwood 1999). Even more significantly, 67% of the teachers reported that constructivism was the *only* teaching approach to which they had been exposed in their methodology courses.

At the same time as constructivist approaches have been promoted, direct teaching methods have been overtly or covertly criticised and dismissed as inappropriate, with the suggestion that they simply don't work and are dull and boring for learners. The message that most teachers appear to have absorbed is that all direct teaching is old-fashioned and should be abandoned in favour of student-centred enquiry and activity-based learning. It will be argued in a moment that this view is dangerously extreme, and that a more effective approach to teaching and learning mathematics involves combining direct teaching with student-centred activities.

The constructivist classroom

At classroom level, constructivist principles are interpreted as requiring activity-based learning, with much use made of group work, discussion and the exchange of ideas (Orton 1994a). The teacher's role becomes much less that of an instructor and much more that of a facilitator for learning.

Lochhead (1991, p. 82) observes, 'One powerful constructivist mode of instruction is student discussion, often in the form of some type of cooperative problem-solving, with or without the supervision of the instructor'. The value of talk among students and between students and an adult for the purposes of constructing meaning is supported by Inagaki, Hatano and Morita (1998) and Mevarech (1999). They suggest that students, through the process of discussion with their peers, seem to be able to pick up new information, adopt new perspectives and accommodate plausible ideas.

Airasian and Walsh (1997) say that it is not yet clear how constructivist methods relate to the learning of different types of subject matter, or whether these methods are equally valid across all curriculum areas. According to Dick (1992), some advocates for constructivism suggest that the theory applies to all domains of learning. He doubts that this is the case, and queries whether constructivism is really a total theory of learning or whether it is actually an instructional strategy appropriate for a particular type of learning outcome. For example, a constructivist approach to enquiry and problem-solving in mathematics makes good sense. But a constructivist 'find-out-for-yourself' approach to the acquisition of basic numeracy, where mastery and automaticity of skills and knowledge are required, does not make good sense.

Some weaknesses in constructivist approaches

While student-centred, enquiry-based learning is written and talked about very frequently, in practice the methods are quite difficult to implement successfully (Carpenter et al. 1989; Noddings 1990; Sowder et al. 1998). Having a theory about how children construct their own meaning does not immediately lead to a clearly defined classroom teaching model. Helping someone to construct meaning is a very difficult process, unlikely to be achieved by a single teaching approach used alone (Nuthall 1999). Providing resources and creating hands-on, experiential and collaborative learning situations will not achieve all that is required in terms of understanding. It is the teacher, acting as facilitator, interpreter and mediator of meaning, who holds the key to successful learning (Bay et al. 1999). However, the facilitating and mediating role is an extremely difficult and demanding one for any teacher to fulfil. It involves much more than merely handing over, to the children, responsibility for learning. Stevenson et al. (1990) point out that lessons requiring children to discover information and construct understanding for themselves actually require a great deal of time and preparation from teachers. A successful lesson based on constructivist principles needs extremely careful planning and more than usual skill in implementation. It is far from certain that all teachers can perform these demanding tasks effectively, or that they have time to plan lessons with the required degree of care and precision.

Some teachers seem to believe that the 'old way' of teaching numeracy skills was totally wrong and the 'new way' is absolutely right, and that children require only the stimulus and the opportunity to learn for themselves. This belief has the potential to create more learning difficulties. Some teachers may abandon all forms of direct teaching and explanation. One must wonder if the 2–3% of students who reported in the TIMSS study that their mathematics teachers never explain how to attempt problems reflects the teachers' misunderstanding of their role. Where this situation occurred, students tended to achieve at much lower levels than did students who received some degree of explanation and demonstration from teachers (Lokan, Ford & Greenwood 1997).

Bjorklund (1995) has warned that although children do develop number sense and basic mathematical relationships without explicit instruction, most mathematical understanding, including simple arithmetic and more complicated concepts, is acquired successfully via formal instruction. Bruner (cited in Wood 1998, p. 228) also argues that explicit instruction is necessary if children are to effectively interpret and understand their learning experiences.

Alexander (1995, p. 31) talks of contemporary teachers having to 'walk the ideological tightrope', balancing a child-centred approach with some degree of teacher-centred instruction. Alexander reminds teachers that, 'While ideology dictates a teacher role of facilitator and encourager, common sense (not to mention recent classroom research) indicates the benefits for children of purposeful intervention by the teacher, especially of a kind which generates cognitive challenge'. Skemp (1989a, p. 86) confirms that knowledge structures have to be built by every learner, but is adamant that 'good teaching can greatly help'. He suggests that the more abstract and hierarchical the content to be mastered, the more teacher help is needed. Similarly, Steen (1999) says that some students and some types of mathematical reasoning may require quite explicit instruction.

Does a constructivist approach suit all learners?

While accepting the importance and value of a well-conducted student-centred approach to learning and teaching, it is essential to consider whether the approach suits all types of learners. Are all students equally capable of 'making meaning' without explicit instruction? The answer seems to be no. Some students appear to make optimum progress and benefit most when exposed to direct teaching and a structured curriculum (Graham & Harris 1994; Mastropieri, Scruggs & Butcher 1997; Tuovinen & Sweller 1999). To such students, discovery approaches used alone can be frustrating and confusing. The situation is captured well in a cartoon showing two children standing next to a maths activity table with one saying to the other, 'All I ever "discover" is that I don't understand it'. Perhaps the most significant difference among learners is their need for more (or less) teacher direction. Souviney (1994) draws attention to the fact that in a class of thirty students involved in constructivist activities, some will respond well and enter strongly into the processes of discussion, questioning and reflecting. Some will perform weakly, leaving most of the work to others and accepting results without question.

Boaler's (1997) study in secondary schools discovered a small but significant group of students who did very little work in open-ended, unstructured mathematics lessons. They seemed reluctant or unable to engage in the necessary self-directed learning and spent time off-task, distracting other students or disturbing the lesson. These students explained their misbehaviour in terms of the lack of direction in the lesson and insufficient guidance from the teacher.

Difficulties in coping with a predominantly or exclusively constructivist approach are not confined to the least able students. Teachers' observations seem to indicate that some quite able students are frustrated by methods that require them to discuss, reflect and analyse. They are more goal-oriented in learning style and aim for quick mastery of content and skills. They too seem to enjoy a more structured and direct approach (A. Watson 1999).

Does a constructivist approach suit all types of learning?

It is important to consider whether a constructivist approach suits all types of learning. Does gaining mastery over the broad range of knowledge, concepts, skills and strategies necessary to become numerate involve only one type of learning? Again, the answer seems to be no. Different learning processes are involved in acquiring facts and concepts from the processes involved in developing intellectual skills and strategies. Gagne, Yekovich and Yekovich (1993) identify three main types of learning applicable to the mathematics domain. They are:

- *declarative knowledge*, such as automatic recall of number facts, understanding of mathematical vocabulary, recognition of symbols, etc.;
- *automated computational skills*, such as performing fluently the algorithms for the processes of addition, subtraction, multiplication and division;
- *cognitive strategies*, which are mental 'plans of action' used for reasoning, hypothesising, problem-solving and self-monitoring.

The first two categories might be regarded as lower-order knowledge and skill. The 'automated computational skills' are part of what some writers refer to as 'procedural knowledge' in mathematics (Baroody 1993). The third category can be considered as representing higher-order thinking and metacognitive strategies. Higher-order processes usually require a foundation of declarative knowledge and automated skills. For example, declarative knowledge comprises much of the raw material needed to carry out the processes of thinking, reasoning and solving problems.

Gagne, Yekovich and Yekovich (1993) also advise on the type of instruction needed to facilitate particular types of learning and to accomplish specific learning outcomes. For example, if automaticity is required then the teaching method must provide abundant opportunities for practice with feedback. To establish a firm base of essential declarative knowledge (recall of basic number facts, for example) and to develop automaticity in computational skills, learners must experience an adequate amount of sustained practice. The old-fashioned way of providing practice was through regular speed and accuracy drills, revision exercises and rote memorisation of multiplication tables. The modern method assumes that students will acquire sufficient facility in basic number knowledge and skills through engaging in problem-solving and enquiry. Although ensuring that lower-order skills are always used in context, the constructivist approach does not ensure that students will acquire essential fluency and automaticity in basic number and in computation.

Combining explicit teaching, practice and student-centred learning

Battista (1999) argues strongly for a meaningful approach to mathematics teaching that encourages reasoning and reflection rather than rote learning, but points out the need to ensure that students become fluent in basic number facts since these are essential for mental computation, estimation and problem-solving. Similarly, Frobisher (1994) confirms that problem-solving usually has to draw upon knowledge and skills that have been perfected through practice exercises.

Both Bishop (1999) and Grant (1998) argue the benefits of clear and direct teaching, with balanced emphasis on computational speed and accuracy as well as on problem-solving and enquiry. Even Noddings (1990), an acknowledged advocate of the constructivist approach, recommends that teachers anticipate some of the basic skills students will need in constructing important concepts and solving problems. To firmly establish these skills, students may require direct teaching and intensive periods of practice so that the skills can be used without effort in solving problems. This is the type of learning that Meadows (1993) refers to as 'automated knowledge' — knowledge that can be recalled without effort when required, allowing maximum cognitive working space for other higher-order processes. Hunter (1994) says that knowing information, processes and procedures so well that they can be applied automatically releases mental effort for dealing with more complex information. Automaticity comes from practice.

This plea for adequate attention to practice and overlearning of the 'basics' is not an argument for teaching a body of decontextualised information prior to using it for real purposes. Lochhead (1991, p. 77) says, 'Perhaps the most poisonous piece of realist dogma corrupting current instruction is the notion that students need to be taught some set of basic facts before they can be asked to think'. He goes on, 'When a set of facts are memorised prior to serious work, that merely means that little thought has gone into their construction and they are therefore ill-defined and poorly constructed'. Rather than suggesting that teachers should teach decontextualised facts, the point is that essential knowledge arising from any learning experience may need to be made more explicit, and practiced thoroughly, if it is to be stored successfully in students' long-term memory. Research has demonstrated quite convincingly that real competence, whether in basic number skills or solving problems, comes only with extensive practice (Steen 1999). Many years ago, at the height of the first 'new mathematics' movement in Britain, Fletcher (1970) wisely remarked that, after activity-based lessons, children must be given plenty of practice to help develop and consolidate what they have learned. He warned, 'It does not follow that children always remember what they discover' (p. 2). The value of automated knowledge is much greater if it has been learned first through application in meaningful contexts.

All this adds up to the need to understand that there are different types of learning, each requiring a different type of teaching. Galton et al. (1999) and Hunter (1994) have advised teachers to select methods of instruction that suit the types of learning involved in a lesson, as well as suiting the age, ability and aptitude of the students. A teaching method should be judged on its 'fitness for purpose'. Unless balance is achieved between direct teaching and activity-based, constructivist approaches, it is most unlikely that reforming mathematics teaching will significantly reduce failure rates. The problem could become one of moving away from too much teacher direction, drill and practice, to too little. In such a situation, the students with learning problems stand to lose most. Vaughn, Bos and Schumm (1997, p. 429) remark:

> Despite the plea for additional emphasis on problem-solving, computation is still an essential component of the mathematics curriculum. Some feel that students with learning problems potentially have the most to lose as the curriculum shifts away from computation … The concern is that because students with learning problems need to learn basic math facts, and because a lack of knowledge of these facts is a common impediment to learning higher-level maths, students with learning problems may learn neither math computation nor higher-order mathematics.

International standards in mathematics

The remaining issue of interest has arisen from the evidence in comparative research studies, such as TIMSS, indicating that the overall standard of mathematics achievement in some countries (including Britain, the US and, to a lesser degree, Australia) is not as high as we would wish (Lokan, Ford & Greenwood 1996; Mullis et al. 1997; Reynolds & Farrell 1996; Robitaille 1997; Stigler & Hiebert 1999). These studies have also shown that attainment levels in mathematics vary significantly in different parts of the world, with students in Hong Kong, Singapore, Japan, and Korea significantly outperforming comparable students elsewhere (Galton et al. 1999; Mullis et al. 1997; O'Brien 1999; Stevenson et al. 1990). The fact that students in some countries achieve much greater success forces us to seek an explanation. Are the superior results due to more effective teaching methods or better instructional resources? Can the achievement level of other students be improved through adopting the teaching strategies used in the countries where high attainment is the norm?

Many reasons for the higher achievement levels have been suggested, including cultural influences and parental expectations in different countries, the teaching methods used, the textbooks and other resources, the amount of time spent on mathematics instruction and on homework, and the degree of outside tutorial support available. There is even a suggestion that the language structures and vocabulary used, for example in counting and in defining concepts, may make learning mathematics easier or more difficult in different countries (Bell 1995).

It is popular to criticise cross-cultural studies for reasons such as international variation in curriculum, research tests not being culture-free, home background and cultural factors confounding attempts to look at the impact of teaching method, samples of students not being representative, and so on. For a summary of the main criticisms, see Chen, Lee and Stevenson (1993) and Reynolds and Farrell (1996). However, regardless of all the potential problems in such studies, Lokan, Ford and Greenwood (1996) consider that there is sufficient evidence to confirm that teaching approach and classroom factors do make a significant impact on students' progress in mathematics. Robitaille (1993) and Reynolds and Farrell (1996) indicate that international comparisons can help evaluate the effectiveness of different approaches to curriculum and to teaching. Perhaps the most important point in relation to international studies is made by Schaub and Baker (1994, p. 164), when they conclude that 'Effective mathematics teaching is not culturally bound. Effective teaching and learning is attainable using sound, proven, and standard methods of classroom management and instruction'.

Teaching approaches in Asian classrooms

Since the 1970s, cross-cultural studies have shown that students in many countries lag behind their Asian counterparts as early as Year 1, and some studies have suggested that the difference becomes more pronounced as the children get older (Mullis et al. 1997; Stevenson et al. 1990; Stevenson & Stigler 1992; Stigler & Hiebert 1997). Taking Japan as an example, Benjamin (1997, p. 20) indicates that 'we are not just talking about schooling that is marginally more effective in Japan than in other countries, but education that is dramatically more effective'.

Due to the measurable success of teaching in Japan and other East Asian countries, their teachers have become the focus of research attention in recent years (Chen, Lee & Stevenson 1993; Sawada 1999; Schaub & Baker 1994; Shimizu 1995; Stigler, Fernandez & Yoshida 1996). Researchers have tried to discover what Asian teachers do in the classroom that may positively affect student achievement. For example, the Third International Mathematics and Science Study was the first time videotape was used to record and study mathematics teachers at work. More than 230 classrooms in Germany, Japan and the US were visited during the study. There were observable qualitative differences in the way instruction was given, the use of available time and the levels of thinking required of students (Stigler & Hiebert 1999).

It is often argued that students in countries scoring highly on numeracy tests in international studies have been drilled in computational skills mainly through rote learning, and are less proficient when it comes to solving problems and applying what they know. The video studies showed, however, that Japanese students actually spent less time than did students in Germany and the US practising routine procedures, and more time analysing data and checking or proving their strategies for solving problems. Stigler and Hiebert (1997) report that Japanese teachers emphasise critical thinking and reflecting. In contrast, US teachers appear to be concerned with only the first two stages of learning (acquisition and application), giving some attention to developing fluency in lower-order computational processes and number facts. Japanese classrooms cover these basic levels thoroughly, but also give due attention to helping students use their knowledge to solve problems and analyse the strategies they have applied. In contrast, US teachers are reported to spend too much time merely getting students to memorise procedural knowledge, rather than developing conceptual understanding (Herman 1994; Ma 1999; O'Brien 1999). As a result, US students are reported to be less proficient in solving problems and applying their knowledge (Silver 1997). Children in Britain are also reported to be less competent in solving problems (Galton et al. 1999).

Most Asian teachers spend a great deal of time preparing maths lessons carefully. They use predominantly whole-class teaching methods, do not spend huge amounts of time revising or going over old work, keep behaviour management and administration time to a minimum and maintain a brisk pace of instruction. The typical mathematics lesson in Japanese classrooms involves four stages:

- a problem is presented;
- students attempt to solve the problem, often working collaboratively with a partner or in a small group;
- there is whole-class discussion about the methods used to obtain an solution;
- the teacher sums up, and the thinking is applied to a similar problem (Shimizu 1995).

One of the key features of lessons observed in Japan is the teacher's explicit summary at the end of a lesson, providing an overview and revision of what has been discovered and how it can be applied (Benjamin 1997).

Teachers in Asian countries seem to present highly coherent and carefully sequenced lessons, and endow their classes with a liveliness and variety that hold students' interest (Stevenson et al. 1990). Benjamin (1997) reports that cohesion, thoroughness and emphasis on understanding as well as skill in calculation are characteristic of Japanese teachers. Chinese and Japanese teachers are reported to have a better conceptual understanding of mathematics themselves, resulting in less reliance on procedural and algorithmic teaching (Ma 1999). Because many teachers are specialists in their subject (they teach only mathematics to a number of different classes even in primary school), they can polish their lessons to perfection. Teachers in other countries, such as Britain and Australia, are generalists at primary-school level, and maths is only one of many different curriculum areas they have to teach each day. They simply do not have time to develop such well-constructed lessons. This could be a problem in a country where constructivist approaches predominate (Robitaille 1997).

Unlike Chinese and Japanese teachers, US teachers lead their class (actively instruct students) for less than half the time allocated to mathematics. The children spend most of their time doing worksheets or other forms of independent work, rather than interacting directly with the teacher. The teacher spends much time moving around the room helping individuals. This is also fairly typical of classrooms in Britain and Australia. It is argued by some observers (e.g. Reynolds & Farrell 1996) that the complex pedagogy employed by teachers in the West, in seeking to cater for individual differences, actually increases these differences over time.

Japanese and other Asian teachers of mathematics seem able to minimise the between-learner variation in attainment, so that the distance between the slowest and fastest learners does not create a major problem (Schaub & Baker 1994). In some countries, such as the US, Britain and Australia, a significant distance between the highest and lowest achievers exists from the early years of schooling and the gap often increases — partly due to the emphasis on individual progression and group work rather than on whole-class teaching.

In most Asian classrooms students spend much less time in routine deskwork. Almost 80% of the available time is spent interacting with the teacher in a whole-class session (Stevenson et al. 1990). In many classrooms most of the work is based on the textbook used by all students or is on the blackboard, so that teachers have to spend less time preparing differentiated worksheets (Benjamin 1997).

Although Japan has a well-established system for providing special educational support to students (LeTendre & Shimizu 1999), most of the help given to individual students occurs in the regular classroom and is delivered by the mainstream teacher. This contrasts with other countries where remedial assistance is often delivered in a withdrawal situation, often at a slower pace and sometimes unconnected with the regular classroom curriculum.

Students' concentration and application to task in Chinese and Japanese classrooms is reportedly much better than in many Western countries, partly because there are fewer distractions of the type that occur with fairly continuous group work and informal methods, but also because the children are given a short break after every 45-minute lesson. The brisk pace of teaching also helps to motivate students and keeps them on-task and productive. Chinese and Japanese children are also taught the self-management skills needed to organise themselves without wasting lesson time, thus ensuring that instructional time is used effectively.

In Taiwan, Hong Kong and Japan strict guidelines define what must be taught and when it must be taught. These guidelines, together with more days in the school year, more hours devoted to mathematics instruction and more time spent on homework, enable teachers to cover much more curriculum content. In general, Asian children spend more hours a week and more days per year doing maths.

Chen, Lee and Stevenson (1993, p. 33) comment:

> What we have found is that Asian teachers apply what everyone would agree are reasonable and thoughtful approaches to presenting mathematics to children. The major difference between what occurs in the East and the West is that Asian teachers appear to apply these approaches with greater consistency and frequency than do their Western counterparts. In doing this, they are helping to produce students who are leading the world in their achievement in mathematics.

Cultural and familial influences

Undoubtedly, not all the superior achievement of Asian children in numeracy can be attributed to teaching methods and curriculum alone. Many factors outside school are also influential. For example, Wong (1993) points out that the majority of Chinese students are influenced by their Confucian cultural heritage, which makes them hard-working and achievement-oriented. This, together with the importance placed by almost all parents on their children's school progress and examination results, puts pressure on students to work very hard. The cultural belief is that hard work can overcome any weaknesses in learning.

Asian children do large amounts of homework. Families expect this and are fully supportive, parents ensuring that the work is done and giving help when needed. Certainly, some of the strength of Asian children's performance may come from their additional hours of practice at home. Also, it is not unusual for students, even the most able, to attend private tutorial classes after school hours.

Clearly, success in becoming numerate depends on factors in school and in children's home background and culture. Chapter 2 examines what is known about children's early learning and the message this knowledge should convey to teachers about effective teaching approaches. Later chapters will explore, in more detail, various aspects of teaching.

The city of Trantuille
exactly 200 km north
Butan is 90 km due e
oximately how far
from Seatown?

2 More on children's learning

algorithms

Using the physical and mental tools they are born with, children interact with their environment to make sense of it, and in doing so, they construct their own mental concepts of the world. The brain seems to be conditioned to take in information about objects and their relationships to one another (Beaty 1998, p. 227).

The quotation reminds us that young children acquire their earliest numerical and mathematical concepts through their spontaneous activity and first-hand experiences. From an early age, most children without disabilities engage in exploration that leads them to discover quantitative features of their environment. For example, actions with building-blocks, construction toys and other materials can lead them to discover spatial relationships and the characteristics of particular objects (Hawthorne 1992). Through meeting more advanced individuals in their social setting they observe and acquire such skills as counting, often through incidental learning and imitation but sometimes as a result of direct teaching. Through play with others they encounter concepts such as shape, relative size, capacity, sharing, sorting and classifying. They begin to compare and contrast groups of objects. Quantitative elements begin to appear in early drawings, suggesting that children are able to invent simple ways of representing number relationships (Pound 1999).

In the early stages, children's level of understanding is linked very closely with the real world. Things that can be handled, and situations that can be experienced directly and are important to them, are most readily understood. Seemingly without direct instruction, young children often devise intuitive strategies for dealing with addition, subtraction and sharing (Whitebread 1995).

There is no doubt that children begin to develop 'number sense' from quite an early age. Some experts suggest that this number awareness is akin to the phonological awareness children develop for the speech sounds they encounter. Just as phonemic awareness is vital for beginning to learn reading and spelling when children enter school, so does 'number sense' seem to underpin their smooth entry into early arithmetic skills (Butterworth 1999; Gersten & Chard 1999).

The role of language

Children refine their understanding of number relationships and other mathematical concepts not only through their actions but also through talking with and listening to others (Lee & Lawson 1996; Stoessiger & Wilkinson 1991). Language is extremely important for interpreting situations, seeking information, conveying meaning and storing information in forms other than purely perceptual, motor and sensory.

The language of others, if used at the appropriate level of complexity, helps children to further interpret a particular mathematical experience and can add to their growing vocabulary. This vocabulary provides some of the raw material for thinking about and communicating simple mathematical relationships. For example, when playing with an adult or older sibling a child may count how many blocks were used to make a model house. The adult may say, 'Wow! You used nine blocks for your house. I think you used more than me. Let's count them. Yes, you used more. I used six. How many more blocks did you use? How could we find out?' In this way, through play, words like 'more' and 'less' are encountered in a meaningful context, and skills of counting and comparing emerge naturally. This vocabulary and the language patterns are used later when the child thinks and reasons in the absence of real objects and first-hand experience.

Many teachers, therapists and parents recognise that, in some children with problems in learning mathematics, part of the difficulty can be traced to limitations in vocabulary and language ability (Grauberg 1998). Staves (1999b) points out that one of the main problems encountered by students with learning difficulties is translating between their own intuitive and concrete understanding of the real world and the language used to describe and quantify for mathematical purposes in school. This situation is most apparent in the case of students with intellectual disability or significantly impaired hearing, but a similar language-processing difficulty is sometimes evident in some students with a learning disability.

The value of discussion

Russian psychologist Lev Vygotsky came to regard children's use of language as essential for mental development (Vygotsky 1962). He viewed formal thinking skills and strategies as mainly the product of language development (Zepp 1989). The Vygotskian approach to learning and teaching stresses the important role of social interaction and dialogue in promoting concept development (Van Oers 1996). Social interactions and discussions help children to make connections between the separate bits of information they acquire through their own actions, observations and reflections (Pound 1999). Early childhood programs today incorporate Piaget's emphasis on active exploration and Vygotsky's views on social interaction and talk, by giving children opportunities to explore and discover on their own as well as to interact with adults who support their efforts and challenge them to make new discoveries (Beaty 1998).

The role of language is of vital importance for the acquisition of basic and higher-order concepts throughout the school years (Greenes, Schulman & Spungin 1992). The language interactions involved in mathematics learning and teaching need to take place between child and child, and between adult and child. Discussion between children is a vital part of deepening understanding, particularly when one child explains something to another child or to an adult (Nuthall 1999; Skemp 1989a). Equally important are teachers' clear explanations of mathematical situations, together with their frequent questioning of children during learning experiences. Activities such as justifying their reasoning, explaining and demonstrating help students to understand and to develop higher-order levels of understanding (Steen 1999). These activities were typical in the most effective classes studied in Asia (see chapter 1).

The important role of language in mathematics learning is reinforced in the *National statement on mathematics for Australian schools* (Australian Education Council 1991, p. 19). It states, 'Students are likely to develop mathematical ideas more readily when they have clear ways of labelling and talking about their experiences'. Brown (1998) observes that one of the most significant characteristics of good numeracy teaching is that it is accompanied by a great deal of classroom discussion that is led by, but not dominated by, the teacher.

The use of talk in mathematics also serves a diagnostic purpose. Teachers can find out more about the level of thinking and the strategies used by children through listening to children's explanations and ideas as they apply numeracy skills and solve problems (Baroody 1993; Lilburn & Rawson 1993). Major clues to students' misconceptions and confusions are revealed most easily in their talk and in the questions they ask. Teachers need to encourage much more discussion than is typical in many mathematics classrooms, and must become skilled listeners (Goulding 1997). Teachers are responsible for ensuring that children have the opportunity to interpret and explain new learning to one another and to adults, talking their way to understanding (Burton 1994b; Flood 1999). In her article 'The twelve most important things you can do to be a better math teacher', Burns (1993) ranks as first helping children to explain the logic of their procedures and the reasonableness of their solutions when they solve problems. One of the strengths of the constructivist approach is that it frequently involves students in 'thinking aloud' while solving problems and manipulating materials. This not only helps the teacher to assess the strategies students are using and their level of thinking, it also helps the students themselves reflect upon whether what they are doing is right or wrong, and what may need to be changed (Souviney 1994).

Writing in mathematics

It is not only oral language that is important for fostering understanding. In recent years much interest has been shown in the value of children's written recordings and communications of mathematical ideas (e.g. LeGere 1991; Morgan 1998; Waters & Montgomery 1993). Writing in mathematics helps students clarify their thinking and make links with other ideas and concepts. The form of writing may be simply 'explaining what you mean', elaborating on how students obtained a solution and the steps they went through, summarising, or generating word problems for others to solve. Waters and Montgomery (1993) and Morgan (1998) believe that trying to write helps students clarify meaning and strengthens their own understanding, particularly in relation to difficult concepts and when solving problems.

Students' written work in mathematics can become part of the collection of work samples included in their portfolios. The role of portfolios in the assessment process is described in chapter 6.

The overall importance of oral and written language in learning mathematics, and the implications of this for teachers, are summed up well by Costello (1991, p. 180):

> Learning mathematics can be seen as a continuous process of making sense, not only of the subject itself, but of the quantitative and spatial aspects of reality. This process demands discussion and negotiation, it relies at times on skills of reading and writing, and ultimately it requires the development of formal language and notation in which abstractions can be made precise. The challenge for the mathematics teacher is to encourage a use of language in the classroom so as to provide a context within which pupils can make mathematical ideas their own.

Moving from concrete to abstract

The first step that most children take in moving from the real world of objects is to use pictorial recordings of number relationships, for example drawing a picture with two big human figures to represent parents and two smaller figures to represent self and sibling, or drawing three representations of goldfish in a tank. At around the same time, children are also able to interpret pictorial representations of groups of objects to establish a number relationship, for example counting the kites in a picture or the number of sheep in a field. When situations are presented to children in pictorial form or are recorded by them as pictures, children can easily relate to them even though they are not the real objects. This is the first stage in moving from concrete experience to symbolic representation. It might be called the beginning of the 'semi-concrete' stage (Heddens & Speer 1995).

At the next stage of development, children can use an object to 'stand for' another real object, for example a wooden block can stand for a car, three blocks can stand for three cars following one another along an imaginary road, and so forth. The blocks don't look like cars, but the idea that a thing can be represented in a different way is established. At the later 'semi-abstract' stage, tally marks (looking even less like the real object) can be used, with children understanding their one-to-one correspondence with the original objects.

Young preschool children begin to invent their own ways of recording quantitative relationships on paper, long before any formal instruction is given (Boulton-Lewis & Tait 1994; Pound 1999). Some preschoolers even begin to add and subtract small amounts mentally if the situation is very real to them and they can easily visualise the items referred to by the questioner (Hughes 1986; Staves 1999b).

Not until children have had these intermediate experiences of translating reality into different forms of semi-concrete and semi-abstract representation are they ready to understand and use symbolic recording (Heddens & Speer 1995). It is believed that some children experience difficulty in learning mathematics because they have been taken too quickly from the concrete stage to the abstract symbolic level of recording. There is a gap in children's understanding if they are forced to operate too soon with symbols and mathematical notation. The use of structural apparatus such as Dienes Multibase Arithmetic Blocks (MAB) equipment, Cuisenaire rods, Unifix cubes or Mortensen Mathematics Materials can help to bridge the gap by providing a visual link between real objects and the symbols that can eventually represent them (Reys et al. 1998). We will return later to the use of apparatus.

Some years ago, Liebeck (1984) suggested that effective learning of mathematics depended upon four opportunities in the learning environment. The four elements were:

- direct experience with materials;
- the language used to interpret, organise and quantify that experience;
- pictures, diagrams and other visual methods of representing and summarising the experience;
- an introduction to the symbol systems that can later represent the experience in a more concise abstract way.

Teachers can remember these important ingredients for effective lessons via the mnemonic 'CELPS': CE = concrete experience, L = language used to discuss and question, P = pictorial methods of recording and S = symbolic representation.

Nuthall (1999) describes five processes involved in assimilating and accommodating knowledge and understanding. The processes are:

- acquiring and clarifying information;
- creating associative links with related knowledge and prior experience;
- integrating new knowledge with old to form a more elaborate network;
- evaluating truth and consistency in the information;
- metacognition and self-monitoring to control the ways in which information is being taken in and used.

Nuthall indicates that these processes occur in three situations, namely during structured classroom activities, through discussion with peers, and privately when children reflect internally upon a particular action or experience.

Much of these comments about children's early learning in mathematics is influenced by the theories of Jean Piaget, Lev Vygotsky, Jerome Bruner and Richard Skemp. It will be useful to indicate very briefly a few of their contributions and, in most cases, the complementary nature of their perspectives.

Piaget's perspectives on children's learning

Piaget's theories (e.g. Piaget & Szeminska 1952), based largely on observation of children engaged in thinking and reasoning activities, have underpinned much of the approach we now identify as constructivism. In Piaget's opinion, children's active explorations of the environment, coupled with increasing physical and neurological maturation, play the most important role in influencing their cognitive development. The value of directly teaching knowledge and skills ahead of children's 'readiness' to learn was thought to be largely a waste of time, likely to achieve little in terms of genuine learning. Most Neo-Piagetians (e.g. Case 1991; Demetriou, Shayer & Efklides 1992) have revised this thinking and believe that, with appropriate experiences and skilled teaching, young children can actually learn much more than Piaget believed possible (Clemson & Clemson 1994; Souviney 1994). Experience and instruction appear to be more important than maturation. Neo-Piagetians believe that the broad knowledge and processes needed to learn and to solve problems are teachable, and that we do not need to await children's biological maturation. In this context, we might note that in many Asian regions, such as Hong Kong, where kindergarten education is available, young children are often exposed to small amounts of formal instruction in the basic skills of writing and number. Is this another factor contributing to their success in school and higher achievements in numeracy?

An important part of Piaget's theory of cognitive development is his notion of 'schemata'. A schema is an integrated mental network comprising everything an individual has learned about something. Skemp (1989a) refers to a schema as a 'knowledge structure' in the mind; Anderson (1984) suggests that every schema represents and summarises the various relationships individuals have discovered among their components of acquired knowledge. For example, in a person's mental schema relating to 'squares', that person has discovered that squares have equal straight sides, their corners are always right angles, they can be any size, they occur in many parts of the built environment, they fall within the category known as 'shapes', they can be constructed accurately on paper using particular techniques, using them within building construction in the three-dimensional world usually requires some type of diagonal bracing to strengthen them, and so on. The person did not acquire all that information at one time. The various items of information have been added at different times as the result of new experiences. Another example is the schema an individual develops about the environment within which they live and work. At first, when individuals move to a new town, their mental 'map' may comprise no more than knowledge of where their flat is in relation to the bus stop or train station. Soon, however, they add knowledge of where the shops are, ways of getting to the park, different bus routes and different routes to take when walking to the cinema and the library. Thousands of schemata are developed over an individual's lifetime, and they are constantly changing and expanding. Piaget used the term 'assimilation' to describe the taking in of new information by learners, and 'accommodation' for the process involved in fitting the new information into what is already known. Learners filter, interpret and adjust information in terms of what they already know, and learning is not merely a process of adding information. It is a process of transforming mental structures (Baroody 1993). Piaget argued that children must continually reconstruct their own understanding of phenomena through active reflection until they eventually achieve an adult perspective.

When new learning does not fit in with prior knowledge (is not accommodated within the existing schemata) it remains a fragment of experience which is easily forgotten, or is very difficult to recall and use when needed. In acquiring numeracy skills, this fragmentation can occur when children are taught new rules or facts out of context. They do not relate them to what they already know and therefore meaningful learning does not occur. Pound (1999) suggests that mathematical learning, like all other learning, depends upon making connections. Brown (1998) indicates that, at its crudest, a mental model of mathematical understanding is made up from 'blobs' and 'links'. A blob is an isolated piece of known information, namely, declarative knowledge. Links are the connections between blobs that children must make if a particular concept or skill is to become firmly established and functional. Many learning difficulties in numeracy stem from a situation where learners have too many isolated blobs which are not linked or consolidated.

Piaget considered that individuals pass through four recognisable stages of development on their way to mature cognitive functioning. At each stage they become better able to process information and develop more comprehensive and flexible schemata. In general, the sequence begins with the most basic ability of very young children to develop motor responses and reactions to sensory input. This is the sensory-motor stage, from birth to about eighteen months in normally developing children. It is followed by two developmental stages, the pre-operational or intuitive (usually from eighteen months to seven years) and concrete operational (from seven years to adolescence). During these stages children can understand and process increasingly complex information if it can be experienced, acted upon and observed first-hand. Lastly, normally developing individuals become able to deal with abstract notions, and to think and reason without the need for first-hand experience. This is the formal operational stage, occurring from middle adolescence into adulthood. Students with developmental disorders or delays, and some with general or specific learning disabilities, usually pass through these stages at a much slower rate than other children. Students with intellectual disability may remain at the concrete level of cognition throughout their adult lives.

Numerous experimental studies have failed to discredit Piaget's overall description of the way in which cognitive development occurs in sequential stages. However, some criticisms of his work have emerged. In addition to the current belief that Piaget underestimated what young children could achieve with expert guidance (Pound 1999), it is also believed that he overestimated what average adolescent students could do in terms of abstract (formal) reasoning. In the first translations and commentaries of Piaget's writings, it is common to find that age eleven or twelve was suggested as the end of the concrete operational level. More recent studies suggest that, in the majority of adolescent students, the level of thinking in subjects such as mathematics and science may remain at the concrete stage until age fifteen or sixteen (Collis & Romberg 1992; Lovell 1978). The early misunderstanding led to an assumption that much of the mathematics teaching in secondary schools can be conducted through textbook examples, chalk and talk, without the visual resources and hands-on experience that younger

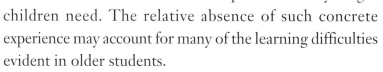
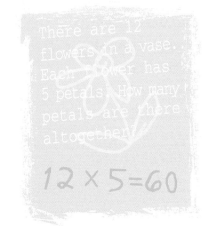

children need. The relative absence of such concrete experience may account for many of the learning difficulties evident in older students.

Piaget's main impact on school curricula and pedagogy has been the recognition that the intellectual capabilities of learners differ appreciably at different ages and that different materials and methods are required for effective learning. For children at the pre-operational and concrete operational levels, active involvement in the mathematics program is vital. Curriculum content at each age level needs to be assessed for its degree of abstraction. Abstraction and the use of purely symbolic representation cannot be forced on children but, as indicated above, it is clear that many young children can carry out simple levels of abstract thinking if the context is one with which they are familiar in real life (Hughes 1986; Pound 1999).

The perspectives of Bruner

Bruner (1960, 1966) was also interested in stages of development and learning, mainly from the perspective of how best to present learning experiences to children. He believed that the sequence of concept development progresses from an 'enactive' stage, in which learning should involve concrete experiences and models, through an 'iconic' stage, where pictorial and other graphic media are used to move beyond the purely concrete, to a final 'symbolic' stage where symbols and abstract notations can convey meaning to learners. His views are not incompatible with those of Piaget, although he was less concerned with issues such as children's 'readiness'. Bruner tended to support the view that young children (and, presumably, slower learners) can be taught most things that other children can learn, if the quality of instruction is good and the teaching follows the sequence of concrete to semi-concrete to abstract levels.

Vygotsky and the 'zone of proximal development'

For many years the writings and thoughts of this Russian psychologist remained relatively unknown to teachers in English-speaking countries. However, recently, his contributions to understanding children's learning and the role of the teacher have been circulated more widely and are appreciated. One of his key notions, the 'zone of proximal development', has emerged as one of the most powerful influences on teaching procedures. It has found a home in what many call 'scaffolded' learning and teaching.

Simply stated, Vygotsky was interested in finding the optimum way of ensuring that children can progress through learning stages smoothly. He observed that children learn best something that they can almost do unaided, but which they haven't quite mastered or have not totally understood. With some guidance or suggestion from an adult or peer they can master the knowledge, skill or strategy quite easily. The help may come from observing a peer or an adult, from being provided with material that makes something more obvious, from being stimulated by pertinent questions or by being directly instructed. The zone of proximal development is the learning distance that students can easily cover if guided directly or indirectly by another person. Gradually, support is phased out so that learners deal with the task independently. Learning activities that fall within a child's zone of potential development have a high probability of success, whereas activities beyond the zone are often too difficult and may result in failure and frustration (Reys et al. 1998).

Two vital ingredients ensure that progress within children's zones of potential development occur in school contexts. One is Vygotsky's insistence that most learning involves social interaction – working with or alongside others. This supports the importance of cooperative and collaborative group work. The second related issue is the importance Vygotsky placed on discussion. McInerney and McInerney (1998, p. 40) comment that:

> An interesting implication of Vygotsky's approach, which stands in contrast to some of the implications that may be drawn from Piaget's theory, is that children should be challenged to be engaged in activities that appear to be beyond their current level of development. Children can often complete activities with the collaboration of teachers and peers that they could not do on their own. In time, with this assistance and verbal mediation, the needed skills are gradually internalised and the children learn to perform them independently.

Given that Piaget may have underestimated what children can do and the potential power of effective teaching, we perhaps need to rethink the popular notion that all curricula should be 'developmentally appropriate' (McInerney & McInerney 1998). Perhaps we are being encouraged to provide experiences too far below children's zones of potential development, rather than providing challenge. Meadows and Cashdan (1988, p. 4) remark, 'We see the best teaching and learning occurring when there are tasks correctly tailored to the child's level and need, which, with the help of an intelligent and experienced expert, the child can handle successfully'.

Skemp: levels of understanding

Skemp's work has much in common with the ideas of Bruner and Vygotsky. Skemp (1989a) believes that physical experiences are the building-blocks from which concepts are extracted by learners. From simple concepts, an effective learner can gradually build more complex and abstract understandings. The teacher's task is to facilitate the acquisition of this meaningful hierarchy of concepts. Skemp acknowledges the importance of discussion and a learner's own language in helping to abstract and focus on key attributes of situations.

One of Skemp's major contributions to the understanding of children's learning is his recognition of at least two levels of understanding within mathematics learning. The first he terms 'instrumental understanding'. Instrumental (or functional) understanding relates to knowledge of what to do and when to do it in terms of selecting the correct information or process to solve a problem or carry out a calculation. At this level learners know what to do but do not necessarily have an in-depth understanding of why or how the procedure works. An example is the application of the rule to invert and multiply when dividing one fraction by another. Many people can remember learning the procedure in school and carrying out the correct steps, but even as adults do not know why it produces the correct solution. There are some advantages in teaching students to acquire a functional/instrumental level of understanding in basic mathematics. These advantages are important for students with learning difficulties. For example, it is easier to teach such students to that level, it gives them immediate rewards in terms of correct solutions, and operating at that level of understanding is usually adequate for everyday purposes.

The second, and potentially more important, level of understanding is what Skemp terms 'relational'. At this level learners fully understand how and why a particular process works, and when to use it. Students who can operate successfully at this level have the following advantages: such understanding allows flexibility in applying strategies to unfamiliar problems, it represents a richer and deeper schema related to that area of learning and experience, all aspects of the schema cohere and make logical sense so they are more likely to be easily remembered, and they provide a consolidated foundation upon which to build further learning.

Skemp (1989a, p. 86) says, 'learning with understanding reduces teacher-dependence and increases personal confidence'. Helping students to establish relational and insightful understanding is a laudable goal in education, but it can be very time-consuming. Ideally, teachers would want to assist all children to achieve both levels of understanding, but it is important to appreciate that even an instrumental level of understanding in numeracy skill is valuable. An individual at that level of understanding knows what to do and when to do it, when working with everyday number situations. A problem arises only if almost all of an individual's learning is at the instrumental level, not well assimilated and not accommodated within cohesive schemata. The learner will eventually have to resort to rote-learning all new material rather than 'intelligent learning', because the essential connections are not being made (Brown 1998).

The cumulative nature of effective learning

Well-consolidated learning builds upon previous learning. Perhaps more than any other area of the curriculum, mathematics depends upon effective connections between new information and prior knowledge and experience. This, not to mention commonsense, suggests that the curriculum in mathematics should be presented in a spiral rather than a linear manner (Reys et al. 1998). By revisiting key ideas and core concepts, applying them each time to slightly more complex situations, learners will surely and smoothly make the necessary links between new knowledge and old competencies.

Developing the beginnings of number sense

At its most basic level, 'number sense' refers to an individual's intuitive feel for the quantitative aspects of the environment. It refers to a simple understanding of numbers and what they represent. A vital component of number sense is the 'cardinal principle': that is, that having carefully counted a group of items, the final number reached actually names the size of the whole set, for example a group of eight. A grasp of the principle of cardinality is essential if a process such as 'counting on' is later to make sense to children. Staves (1999a) considers acquisition of cardinality a milestone in children's early mathematical development. At a higher level, number sense includes the ability to calculate correctly, to appreciate place value, to estimate, to detect errors by recognising when a result is reasonable or unreasonable, and to look at the world and make quantitative comparisons. Baroody (1993) stresses that a primary-school mathematics curriculum should emphasise the development of number sense, including estimation of quantities, measurement and meaningful computation.

Most children enter formal schooling with some number sense (Hughes 1986). Their preschool experience in sorting and grouping, sharing, comparing, counting and one-to-one matching of familiar objects, has led to incidental learning of many of the basic concepts underpinning the mathematics and arithmetic they will meet in school (Heddens & Speer 1995). Even though there is much more to mathematics than number, it can be argued that number concepts and skills provide the foundation upon which most later mathematical thinking and performance relies (Gersten & Chard 1999; Steen 1997).

Although many children can count before they begin school, this does not include children with developmental delays and intellectual impairment (Staves 1999a, 1999b) or some young children from lower socioeconomic backgrounds (Griffin, Case & Siegler 1994). Accurate counting of objects is one of the first things that many students with severe learning problems need to be taught.

Griffin, Case and Siegler (1994) suggest that most preschool children appear to have developed a mental schema or central conceptual structure that allows them to understand simple number relationships. The main components of such a schema appear to be knowledge of the number sequence from one to ten, simple cardinal (group) values, one-to-one counting (word to object), and the idea of 'one more than' or 'one less than'. They have demonstrated that, in children who lack it, it is possible to develop this schema through specific training and experience. The benefits transfer to other areas of basic number work and are evident at least one year after intervention. Their program involves games using dice, number lines, counters and numerals to develop and reinforce basic number knowledge. The aim is to teach children to count accurately forward and back, quantify sets and match sets to numerals. Most of these simple skills and concepts form the basis upon which logico-mathematical knowledge is built (Kamii 1994; Wood 1998). The games involve the children in group work and much discussion and checking of each other. Wood (1998) suggests that a child's grasp of one-to-one correspondence provides the necessary logical basis for counting, adding and subtracting, and that in the early years children begin informally to understand ideas such as 'two for one', providing a basis for concepts of multiplication and ratio.

Sophian (1996) indicates that Piaget considered counting skill was of little value for cognitive development because he believed that children mastered it by rote and did not arrive at an understanding of its value through their own activity and effort. There was some suggestion, for example, that counting did not help with the establishment of conservation of number. This view is no longer accepted and it seems obvious that counting is one way of determining the equivalence of two groups of items, regardless of the way in which the items are arranged (Staves 1999b).

Early development of other mathematical schemata

Number is one area of learning that appears to commence very early in life, but experiences in the other domains of mathematics also occur in the preschool years.

In particular, children acquire a rudimentary understanding of mass, shape and size. For example, they discover that small shapes can often be placed inside (contained within) other larger shapes, and that new shapes can be created by joining shapes together. They discover that some objects that look large feel lighter than some smaller objects, and so on. Through their own actions and observations they will develop schemata relating to assembling objects, transporting objects, positioning objects relative to one another, orientation, horizontality, verticality, enclosure, circularity, ordering, corresponding, capacity, mass and many more (Pound 1999). They will also begin to develop schemata

relating to time and to linear measurement. Rich preschool experiences and the experiences provided deliberately in kindergartens help children to obtain a broader range of mathematical concepts than experiences gained in less stimulating environments.

Chapter 3 considers how these early foundations can be utilised in the further development of numeracy. In particular, it considers some of the ways in which basic numbers skills can be taught.

3 Improving numeracy: general teaching principles and practices

> It is comparatively easy to provide a fertile environment and make it the responsibility of the learner to grow in it. To take on a fair share of the whole teaching–learning process, to teach somebody something that they do not already know is really rather difficult (Meadows & Cashdan 1988, p. 4).

Chapter 2 described some of the important early learning that occurs before children are exposed to instruction in school. We could argue that the experiences children have long before they enter school create the foundation for the success of their numeracy learning in school. Whether the transition from informal to more formal ways of experiencing mathematics is smooth and easy greatly depends on the quality of the teaching and the relevance of the curriculum. It has already been mentioned that many children find 'school maths' so unrelated to their own life experiences and intuitive uses of everyday number that they fail to make a connection between the two (Whitebread 1995). Some learning failure begins at this point. For this reason it is important to consider the features of effective teaching and the ways in which children's encounters with mathematics in school can be made both relevant and successful.

This writer believes that good-quality teaching of numeracy involves a very skilful blend of explicit teaching, student-centred activity, enquiry, discovery, discussion, relevant practice and meaningful application. As Brown (1998) succinctly puts it, the three elements necessary for effective learning in mathematics are:

- active teaching;
- making sense;
- practice.

This chapter explores some of the evidence that supports a balanced approach which combines these essential ingredients. It will argue that not only is balance necessary, but that the balance must reflect what we know about different types of learning and different characteristics of students.

Effective teaching

Alexander (1995) suggests that effective classroom interaction and discourse leading to successful learning combines three main elements, namely:

- direct teaching that instructs children in what to do and how best to do it, and that checks for learning;
- enquiry, that poses problems and offers a challenge to children's thinking;
- scaffolding, that comprises a form of indirect support to help children build on their current level of understanding and develop some independence in their learning.

Alexander's notion of scaffolding derives directly from the work of Vygotsky (discussed in chapter 2) and relates to his concept of children's 'zone of proximal development'. Scaffolding refers to the suggestions, questions, information and ideas that the teacher or a peer might provide to help learners acquire a level of understanding that they would not have achieved unaided. Such scaffolding appears to be essential for stimulating higher-order cognitive skills (Galton et al. 1999) and will be discussed in more detail in chapter 5, on teaching problem-solving strategies. The other two elements in Alexander's list also reflect the desirable balance between instruction from the teacher and student-centred learning. One without the other does not constitute a totally effective teaching approach.

In addition to Alexander's three basic principles, Lilburn and Rawson (1993) have recommended that teachers should:

- base their numeracy teaching on real situations;
- choose activities relevant to the children's experiences;
- use activities related to the children's interests;
- select a variety of different materials and resources;
- encourage children to tackle problems in their own way;
- be flexible in the way children are grouped for different activities;
- listen to what children have to say, since this provides valuable insights into their thinking;
- encourage children to take risks and to learn from their errors.

Brown (1998) has indicated that for children to understand and enjoy mathematics, relate it to real life and perform well, they need experiences that will help them to:

- recognise links between prior knowledge and new information;
- practice and consolidate recall of basic facts;
- store new learning in a form that is easily retrieved when needed;
- explain, discuss and describe the work they are doing and the ideas they are developing;
- be exposed to a range of teaching styles and experiences.

Teaching for higher achievement

There is no shortage of information about the types of teaching that are correlated most highly with good student attainment. For example, in Britain the Office for Standards in Education (OFSTED 1993) reported the results from observation of 384 mathematics lessons across 128 primary schools. The conclusion was that good standards were most evident in classes where the teacher used a variety of methods to teach knowledge, skills and understanding. In those classes students received a fair degree of direct teaching, including explanations and questioning to deepen their thinking, and much group and whole-class discussion. Time was used effectively to engage students throughout the lessons. Less successful classes were typified by work that was poorly planned and executed, often with much time lost through attending to organisation and administration matters rather than to instruction.

OFSTED (1993, p. 7) produced the following useful list of characteristics of classes that achieved the best learning outcomes in mathematics. Teachers used:

- well-planned work with clear lines of progression based upon sound assessment of the students' abilities;

- an appropriate balance of whole-class, group and individual work;

- teaching which enabled children to talk confidently about number, to ask and respond to relevant questions and to receive clear explanations about number operations and relationships;

- a brisk pace of learning, achieved through setting and monitoring clearly defined tasks;

- mental work, including the learning of tables and number facts and involving, whenever appropriate, the application of number skills to real-life problems;

- purposeful investigation which strengthened students' understanding of number patterns and relationships, often through work in other subjects such as science or technology;

- consistent and constructive marking of work, including clear analysis of errors and what needed to be done to correct them;

- well-organised classrooms in which the teacher and students made effective use of a range of printed and practical materials, and achieved a good mix of mental, oral, practical and written number activities.

An analysis of some of the data from the Third International Mathematics and Science Study (TIMSS) suggests that variety and balance in teaching approach are important and are related to achievement in mathematics (Lokan, Ford & Greenwood 1996, 1997). For example, in classrooms where no use is made of group work or where no projects or thematic studies in mathematics are undertaken, the measured attainment level tends to be lower than in classrooms where some (but not excessive) use of these approaches is made.

However, the attainment level is also lower in classrooms where group work, projects and thematic studies are the dominant approach and are used most of the time. The message seems to be that some appropriate use of group work and projects is useful, but too much or too little of both can have a negative impact on learning. Exactly the same situation exists with classroom testing, students' use of calculators, and teachers' explanations and demonstrations of how to carry out calculations. Some use of these tactics can be helpful, but too much has a negative impact on achievement. This must be remembered by those who advocate student-centred, activity-based methods and group work as the only way to develop mathematical concepts and skills.

Extremists who advocate exclusive use of student-centred enquiry and activity methods to foster mathematical understanding may feel uncomfortable with the fact that research results have given significant support to the value of whole-class teaching. Chapter 1 showed that in most Asian countries where attainment levels are high, much of the instruction is of the whole-class variety — but not of the passive 'chalk-and-talk lecture' type. The term 'interactive whole-class teaching' is a better description of the way in which the teaching takes place (Galton et al. 1999). Adhami (1999) and Mullis et al. (1997) point out that whole-class teaching can be very efficient as well as effective, mainly because less time is lost in management and administration of group work and in setting and supervising individualised assignments. Teachers can make presentations, conduct discussions, demonstrate, summarise and stimulate the group most effectively (Sawada 1999). This is not an argument against group work, but an indication that working in groups should not be the only way for students to encounter mathematics.

Research evidence on effective instruction

In what was at the time an extremely comprehensive review of effective teaching approaches in mathematics, Lloyd and Keller (1989) reported much that mirrored the more general research evidence on teacher effectiveness. For example, they found that effective instruction included clear explanations and demonstrations by the teacher, guided practice with feedback to the students, independent practice, frequent revision of previously taught material, and regular monitoring of the children's learning. Clarity of instructions and explanations, appropriate pacing of the lesson, a positive classroom atmosphere and clear objectives have also been recognised as features of effective teaching (Killen 1996; Sabornie & deBettencourt 1997). Classrooms run on these lines not only tend to have higher achievement rates, but also much lower failure rates. The gap between higher achievers and lower achievers tends not to increase over time, as it does with more open-ended approaches. This is reflected in the studies of Asian classroom practices already described (see chapter 1).

In general, the research on teacher effectiveness in the area of mathematics instruction supports the use of a structured approach with a carefully sequenced program. Evidence seems to indicate that effective teachers can provide systematic instruction in mathematics in such a way that understanding can accompany the mastery of basic skills and problem-solving strategies with a minimum of confusion. As we have seen from the example of Asian teachers and exemplary teachers in other parts of the world, successful teachers are good at constructing a sequence of lessons that ensure that students engage with the curriculum material in a stimulating and rewarding manner. Their lessons are typically clear, logical, accurate and rich in examples drawn from the students' own experiences. Rather than merely acting as a facilitator and encourager of children's independent learning, these teachers take an active role in imparting information and skills while still providing ample opportunity for active participation by students. In such an approach, explicit teaching, practical activities, collaborative group work, discussion, practice and application all have a place.

The vital importance of clarity in instruction

Clarity in instructing, explaining and questioning students appears to be a vital ingredient of good teaching. Sotto (1994) suggests that clarity seems to stem from the teacher's thorough grasp of the subject matter, ability to see the subject from the novice learners' point of view, ability to explain in simple terms and ability to relate new concepts to children's own experiences.

While some constructivists regard explanations as a form of transmission teaching, Pressley and McCormick (1995, p. 7) emphasise that 'direct explanation is a decidedly constructivist approach … students do not passively learn from the explanations but rather actively learn from them'. A good, clear explanation can be just what learners require in order to assimilate and accommodate new information into the relevant schema, and to link prior knowledge with new understandings. A well-timed, clear explanation provides the necessary amount of scaffolding for the students to make meaning.

Serna and Patton (1997) suggest that a major reason for students' difficulties is lack of clarity when teachers instruct, set tasks for students to attempt, ask questions or explain. They advise teachers to pay particular attention to the level of complexity in their language and the types of examples they select to illustrate a topic. Lack of clarity often arises from the use of complex terminology, failure to draw analogies or examples to which students can relate, giving only verbal explanation without visual or concrete support, and presenting too much information at one time.

The role of questioning in effective learning

Kauchak and Eggen (1998) state that questioning is the most widely used teaching strategy in most classrooms. Questioning is used to motivate, instruct, diagnose and manage students' learning. They also cite research to indicate that teachers' frequent use of questioning is positively correlated with higher achievement. Teachers in classes with the highest achievements ask many questions during their lessons, but proportionately fewer questions that yield incorrect responses or no response from students.

Manouchehri and Goodman (1998), in a classroom observation study, note that 'traditional' (algorithmic) type teachers ask mainly lower-order questions, often answered with yes or no, whereas innovative teachers ask more challenging questions that require a more thoughtful and extended response. Innovative teachers seem to use students' responses more skilfully as a way of diagnosing learners' levels of understanding or misunderstanding.

Although teachers need to ask some challenging questions in order to develop children's higher-order thinking, not all questions should be of this type, particularly in classes containing students with learning difficulties. It has been demonstrated that children with poor learning skills and lack of confidence seem to benefit most from instruction that includes a high percentage of simple, direct questions that focus on the core content of the lesson. It is as if answering these questions helps to consolidate a student's grasp of the topic. These core questions are often referred to as 'lower-order', and it has even been suggested that in mixed-ability classes well over half the questions asked should be of this type. If students are struggling to assimilate basic information, it is usually wise to ask more questions from the lower-order category. Asking too many difficult questions can cause feelings of failure and frustration in students with learning problems.

Teachers are also wise to use the evidence from the classroom research of Rowe (1986) indicating that increased 'wait time' sometimes must be allowed for some students to formulate an answer. Instead of passing quickly to another student if the first does not immediately answer, staying with the first for a few seconds, perhaps rephrasing the question or providing a prompt or cue, allows that student to respond. Extra wait time (only three seconds or so) produces a number of benefits, including an increase in the participation and success rate of lower-ability students.

Since asking questions is such a central teaching function in mathematics classes, teachers need to become highly skilled in questioning techniques. In general, Clopton's (1992, p. 30) advice is the guiding principle: 'Ask questions that build confidence'.

The place of group work in numeracy learning

Too much group work activity in mathematics lessons can result in poorer achievement levels, but the strategic use of some group work is essential in an effective, balanced approach to mathematics teaching. Studies have shown that lessons that include a measure of cooperative group work can facilitate student learning and increase motivation (Abele 1998; Good, Mulryan & McCaslin 1992). Group activities that involve students in discussion and sharing ideas appear to help individuals arrive at a better understanding of key concepts and strategies. Group work, if well-organised and well-managed, can be of particular benefit to students with learning difficulties (J. Watson 1999). Obviously, the tasks and activities must be appropriate for collaborative endeavour. Much that passes for group work in many classrooms is actually individual work carried out in a grouped seating arrangement (Hastings & Schwiesco 1995; Lyle 1996).

According to Gooding and Stacey (1993), factors that facilitate learning in groups include:

- adequate prior knowledge of the topic to enable each member to participate and contribute;
- receiving adequate explanations or feedback from others when required;
- the ability and willingness to listen to other students;
- having an assigned role and responsibility within the group.

Sometimes groups can be based on student ability and aptitude, but at other times the groups should be mixed to allow those with less mathematical ability to interact with those who have more. While ability grouping is quite common in mathematics (often justified by the argument that it facilitates instruction at different levels), Prichard and Bingaman (1993) point out that ability grouping often results in widening the gap in performance between higher and lower achievers, and can dishearten students in the lower-ability groups. It is reported that rigid ability grouping that stresses differences in ability and performance can have negative effects on students with learning difficulties (Wiliam, Boaler & Brown 1999). It is essential to have flexible grouping systems if they are to assist in meeting the needs of all students (Marsh 1999).

Students do not all gain the same value from a group activity. Often one member gets much less from the experience than do the others. Some students tend to be passive and allow the other members to make the decisions and do most of the work. Many students need to be taught how to be useful and contributing members of a group. Goulding (1997) suggests that group work is most successful when:

- specific tasks are assigned to each member of the group;
- targets are set and time limits made clear for each phase of the activity;
- the teacher intervenes, or for a time operates as a contributing member of the group, modelling appropriate listening and collaborative behaviours;
- the students are given time to explain to one another and to share ideas.

The success of group work depends on classroom organisation, the nature of the activities and the composition of the groups. Too often, group work becomes chaotic and does not achieve its goal because the tasks are too vague or too complex, the students are not well-versed in group-working skills, or the resources are not sufficient or appropriate. Careful planning and close monitoring are required if group work is to achieve the desired educational and social outcomes. Sowder et al. (1998) report that activity-based group work can sometimes result in much wasted lesson time through irrelevant discussion by students; even teachers sometimes lose sight of the academic goals of the lesson.

The type of classroom organisation at any given time should be considered in terms of the type of learning involved in a task. Some types of learning outcome are achieved best by group work interaction and discussion, other types through individual quiet work or by whole-class instruction.

The use of peer tutoring

Peer and cross-age tutoring have been fairly widely used to enhance literacy skills development, and Baroody (1993) also reports positive outcomes from establishing classroom situations where one student assists another in mathematics. The value of peer assistance is well-documented (e.g. Cole & Chan 1990; McCoy 1995).

Some advantages of using peer assistance are that:

- it can be less threatening to the student being helped than if the teacher singles him or her out for extra attention in class;
- the peer may be able to see the difficulty or the subject matter more easily from the learner's viewpoint;
- the peer may be able to explain in language more easily understood by the learner and to use examples to which the learner can relate;
- the learner may be more willing to say to the peer-tutor than to the teacher that he or she still does not understand and needs to be shown something again.

Tutoring another student has benefits for the tutor as well as for the learner. Having to teach something to someone else helps to deepen one's own understanding of the subject and to reveal one's own areas of weakness (Ploetzner et al. 1999; Skemp 1989a). However, Lochhead (1991) draws attention to the fact that much typical tutoring, both with adults and with peers as tutors, is too didactic. The tutors do not encourage the learners to think and to work strategies out for themselves, but rather simply to follow instructions and rote-learn new tricks.

Adapting instruction to individual differences

It has been the policy or philosophy for some years in many education systems to advocate mixed-ability grouping of students in most subjects. Rightly or wrongly, mathematics is often seen as the most problematic subject area in this respect, with a significant number of teachers believing that the most effective way to teach maths is to have reasonably homogeneous classes. It is argued that if the ability range in the class is too wide it is impossible, other than by complicated subgrouping within the classroom, to allow for the fact that some students are still struggling with the basics while others need to be extended, challenged and generally taught at a faster rate. It is felt that mathematics, perhaps more than any other subject, is more sequential and hierarchical in nature, and any inability to cope with the most basic work makes it virtually impossible to be successful with higher-order concepts and skills.

In most countries surveyed in TIMSS one of the two main challenges that teachers felt they faced was the problem of different ability levels within the class (Mullis et al. 1997). The second was not unrelated: it was concern about large class sizes. For this reason, in many schools (where student numbers and available resources allow) mathematics classes still tend to be organised by ability, with the most-able learners in the 'top set' (advanced), average students in the middle set (standard), and students with learning difficulties usually in the bottom set (basic or remedial). This book does not intend to debate the relative merits or otherwise of ability grouping. Since the general policy direction is toward mixed-ability classes it is worth considering briefly some of the ways in which curriculum content, resources and methods of instruction can be adapted to cater more effectively for mixed-ability classes.

The term 'differentiation' is often used to describe this adaptive approach to meeting individual needs. Several writers have outlined strategies teachers might use to accommodate individual differences among students (e.g. Conway 1996; Hoover & Patton 1997; James & Brown 1998; Tomlinson 1995), but it is emphasised here that in general teachers do not find differentiation easy to implement in practice (Fuchs & Fuchs 1998; Scott, Vitale & Masten 1998). When students are ability-grouped for mathematics it appears that many consider that differentiation is not required (Wiliam, Boaler & Brown 1999).

Like many ideal educational innovations, differentiation is more talked and written about than actually applied by the average teacher. However, with the increasing trend toward including students with quite significant difficulties and special needs in regular classrooms, the need for some degree of differentiated and adaptive teaching is likely to increase rather than decrease (Lipsky & Gartner 1998). It

is therefore worth summarising the 'standard' adaptations that effective teachers make in order to ensure that more students are understanding mathematics and feeling successful. Teachers might consider the following instructional modifications:

- making greater use of visual aids, concrete materials and practical demonstrations;
- simplifying and restating instructions for some students;
- setting shorter-term objectives for certain students;
- providing more (or less) direct assistance to some students;
- asking questions of different degrees of complexity, ensuring that less-able students are asked many questions they can answer;
- selecting or making alternative curriculum resource materials, including using different textbooks within the same classroom;
- monitoring the progress of some students more closely during the lesson, and re-teaching where necessary;
- setting students different forms of homework. For some this may be additional practice at the same level, for others it will be extension work;
- encouraging peer assistance and peer tutoring;
- making regular and appropriate use of group work, enabling students of different abilities and aptitudes to collaborate.

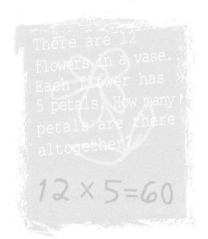

Another suggestion often found in the literature on adaptive teaching is to reduce and simplify the curriculum content that students with learning difficulties have to cover, and slowing the pace of instruction. Caution has to be exercised in acting on this type of advice. Reducing the curriculum and slowing the pace of instruction usually guarantees that a student will fall even more rapidly behind the average level of mainstream students. This may simply create new problems to take the place of the difficulties that existed when there was no differentiation. Whenever possible, the adaptations made in the teaching of mathematics should aim to help the less-able student understand and succeed with the regular program, rather than replace it with a different program. Chapter 1 said that the approach often taken in Asian classrooms is to do everything possible to keep the gap between higher and lower achievers to a minimum, and that this is best accomplished through delivering a common curriculum using mainly high-quality, interactive, whole-class teaching, not complicated systems of individualised programming.

A final word on the use of structural apparatus

One of the main ways of helping children, particularly those with learning difficulties, move from a concrete level of thinking and reasoning to a more abstract level is to introduce them to some form of structural apparatus. Structural apparatus is teaching material designed to embody and clearly illustrate a particular principle, such as number patterns, multiples, factors, place value, ratio, fractional parts etc., or to model an attribute such as relative size or shape. Examples of structural apparatus include Cuisenaire rods (designed by Caleb Gattegno in the 1950s), the Multibase Arithmetic Blocks (MAB) created by Zoltan Dienes, and the interlocking plastic cubes and supporting equipment such as number track and pattern boards known by the brand name Unifix.

In theory, using such material provides a bridge between concrete experience and abstract reasoning by taking learners through experiences at the intermediate levels of semi-concrete (not the real object, but another object or picture used to represent it) to the semi-abstract (the use of the first stages of symbolic representation such as tally marks, used alongside the apparatus) (Heddens & Speer 1995).

It is also argued that the use of structural apparatus helps learners to store visual representations of number relationships and patterns which later help with the visualisation required in abstract reasoning and problem-solving. Burton (1994b, p. 40) refers to this as 'seeing mathematics'. This is particularly the case with equipment such as MAB that helps to illustrate place value clearly; for example, as we move from right to left in a number in base ten the relative value of an item in each column is ten times greater. Apparatus used as a teaching aid can also help to make the key information in word problems more concrete and visual (Marsh & Cooke 1996). For this reason the use of structural apparatus is believed to be particularly valuable for students with learning difficulties (Clayton 1999).

The use of apparatus is certainly not foolproof in helping students acquire understanding. Booker et al. (1997) and Orton (1994b) warn that although the use of such material is widely advocated in schools it often fails to achieve its objectives. The children, for various reasons, fail to connect the activities they carry out with the material to the mathematical principles or concepts the teacher wants them to discover. Sometimes the fault may be with the teacher's instructions or explanation. As Dienes (1964) pointed out many years ago, even when apparatus is used, the links between what is being modelled and the relevant symbolic representation may not be understood by the learners. The teacher may, even while using the structural apparatus, inadvertently resort to 'symbol manipulation tricks' which are not embodied in the model. Sometimes the students become preoccupied with an irrelevant aspect of the material.

It must be recognised that structural apparatus has to be used effectively if students are to focus on the underlying principles rather than the surface features of the material. For example, if structural apparatus is merely being used as an aid to counting then its value is not being fully exploited.

Another problem arises if students come to rely too much on the apparatus for counting, grouping or comparison purposes and do not make the transition to the equivalent mental operations (Thelfall 1996). Teachers must be aware that the apparatus will not necessarily do the teaching for them, and their role is to orient students' attention to salient features through modelling, questioning, explaining and having the students explain what they are doing and the connections they can see.

Even with these reservations, however, Reys et al. (1998, p. 45) conclude that 'research indicates that lessons using manipulative materials have a higher probability of producing greater mathematical achievement than do lessons without such materials … Handling the materials appears to help children construct mathematical ideas and retain them'.

In chapter 4, attention will be given to the teaching of basic number skills with understanding. Some of the general principles of teaching discussed above will be related to specific aspects of numeracy development.

4 Teaching basic number skills

> Computational competence remains important for two valid reasons: (a) it is valuable for determining correct answers in problem-solving tasks and (b) it helps a person determine the reasonableness of responses in everyday situations (Serna & Patton 1997, p. 343).

Number skills underpin almost all operations in mathematics, so helping children establish a firm and confident grasp of these skills is an essential aspect of all school mathematics curricula. Although number skills do not constitute all there is to know about mathematics, they do comprise a very large component. Instruction in basic number must therefore be given high priority within the classroom program (Sabornie & deBettencourt 1997).

For general purposes, number skills include such competencies as:

- counting;
- reading and writing numbers;
- using the four basic processes of addition, subtraction, multiplication and division;
- understanding the concept of equivalence;
- understanding place value;
- estimating;
- recognising numbers in different forms, for example common fractions, decimal fractions and percentages;
- interpreting the signs, symbols and notations associated with operations using numbers;
- using a calculator;
- demonstrating 'number sense'.

Additional information on the body of knowledge and skill constituting basic numeracy is presented in the *National statement on mathematics for Australian schools* (Australian Education Council 1991).

The importance of counting

Chapter 2 indicated that counting (forward and backward) is a very important skill that provides a foundation for numeracy development. For most young children, counting skills are acquired largely through incidental learning during their preschool years. In their daily lives children are surrounded by situations that require them to exercise skills in counting and comparing. The ease with which most children learn to count has been the focus of interest in much of the research into emergent numeracy. Butterworth (1999) even suggests that from birth human brains seem to be 'preprogrammed' to learn counting responses in the same way that brains appear to be prepared for early language acquisition.

Many children can rote-count to ten or even twenty when they enter kindergarten (Payne & Huinker 1993). They may not be accurate in counting actual groups of objects, but they can recite numbers in the correct sequence. This may not be the situation, however, for children whose preschool experiences have been extremely limited, or who are themselves developmentally delayed. On entry to school, such children may have no obvious concept of number, may exhibit no ability to rote-count and may have no number recognition skills.

If children do not yet have the skill of accurate counting it must be directly and explicitly taught. The problem is often that children fail to make a correct one-to-one correspondence between the spoken number 'name' and the objects touched in the group. If the physical act of counting a set of objects appears difficult for a child, manually guiding his or her hand to touch each object as an accompaniment to the oral counting sequence may be helpful.

To count items accurately and meaningfully children must understand at least the following four principles (Ginsburg 1989):

- the counting words must be said in their correct order;
- each item in the set must be counted once and only once;
- each number word must be matched to a separate item;
- the final number reached identifies the total number of items in the group.

The beginnings of addition

There are, of course, several different counting strategies that children can employ once they have moved beyond the simple level of counting a small single group of objects (Leutzinger 1999). For example, given two small groups of known size to be added a child may:

- still begin by counting all the items in the groups starting from 'one' (the 'count-all' strategy);
- start with the larger number and simply count on the smaller number (the 'min' strategy);

- retrieve a known number fact from memory without the need to count on or back;
- retrieve a fact from memory (e.g. 5 + 5 = 10) and adjust it up or down to suit the particular case (e.g. 5 + 6 will be one more than 10);
- carry out the addition using a calculator.

Research studies appear to indicate that these strategies are largely developed by students independently of any explicit instruction, and the strategy a child uses at the time may be fairly resistant to outside modification (Hopkins 1998). It is clear, however, that when students cling to a relatively inefficient procedure for simple number operations, they need to be taught a more efficient system. This writer has found that it is possible, for example, to teach the 'min' strategy to children with learning difficulties who are used to using the less efficient 'count-all' approach.

Without easy recall of basic number facts, students have difficulty with even simple mental addition and subtraction problems. Some authorities (e.g. Payne & Turner 1999) attribute the difficulties that a few students have in carrying out mental arithmetic to limitations in short-term memory. It is argued that these students have difficulty in retaining the several items of information in working memory long enough to make use of them, and therefore become confused. On the other hand, some students have difficulties with simple number processes simply because they have not had sufficient practice and the responses have not become automatic.

Much useful advice on developing the counting-on, counting-up and counting-back strategies can be found in *Teaching mathematics to students with learning disabilities* by Bley and Thornton (1995). Also valuable is the article 'Strategies for basic facts instruction' by Isaacs and Carroll (1999). They point out that mastery of number facts does not conflict with contemporary constructivist views on mathematics learning, since simple number relationships provide the raw material needed for operating with real problems.

Developing automaticity with number facts

Students who continue to employ time-consuming methods for quite simple number operations will be extremely slow when completing longer calculations and solving problems. The message for teachers is that students should be exposed to different ways of manipulating simple numerical information so that the process can be carried out with increased automaticity.

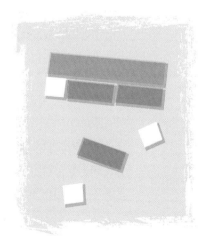

Assisting recall

Some enjoyable number games and computer programs can be used for additional practice and overlearning to ensure that basic number facts are stored more effectively in long-term memory. This work is carried out in parallel with problem-solving and other applications in mathematics. The skills practised should

be related as far as possible to those the students require for everyday use in the broader mathematics curriculum. Serna and Patton (1997) have commented that drill and practice are essential to mastering certain mathematical skills, and many students with learning problems appear to need more practice than do other students. It is important, however, to point out that meaningless rote-practice of number facts is of limited value and potentially very boring. Isaacs and Carroll (1999) suggest that well-managed practice should be designed to develop students' expertise and confidence. It should be brief, engaging, purposeful and distributed over time.

Many students, after the normal amount of practice and application, can recall number facts and processes without particular effort. However, some students with learning difficulties, particularly those with short-term memory limitations, may need to be taught to use specific strategies for storing and retrieving such information. One such approach is to increase the attention students give to storing visual, rather than aural, images. For example, some children may find it easier to remember 3 x 8 = 24 if they can remember what this pattern looks like when made up from three Cuisenaire rods, rather than trying to recall the verbal information that 'three times eight equals twenty-four'. Students appear to differ in the extent to which they spontaneously use visual imagery to store information. It is possible that encouraging them to make greater use of visual strategies will assist their recall.

One learning technique ('look–cover–write–check'), often used to improve recall of spelling patterns in language lessons, can also be applied to mastering specific number facts. The approach capitalises on visualisation as a strategy for remembering the number facts (Sheffield & Cruikshank 1996). The facts selected are usually those which diagnostic assessment shows have not been mastered. For example, if a student can't recall that 9 x 8 = 72, it is possible that encouraging visual imagery by using a flashcard displaying this number fact will help the student to take a 'mental picture' of the information and store it as a visual image in long-term memory (Stading, Williams & McLaughlin 1996).

Greene (1999) has experimented successfully with flashcards containing amusing visual cues to help students with learning disabilities recall specific number facts, for example a picture showing 'sticks [six] in heaven [seven] with a warty shoe [forty-two]' to trigger recall of 6 x 7 = 42. Such mnemonic tricks appear to help some learning-disabled students remember important information; but obviously it is an approach based on rote memorisation rather than meaningful learning and for that reason should be seen as a last resort.

For students with learning difficulties, more than the ordinary amount of time and attention must be given to what Grauberg (1998) refers to as 'maintenance drills', to ensure that number facts and routine procedures become firmly established. This makes them available for appropriate use with speed and accuracy in problem-solving (Steen 1999). Resources to help with this type of practice are listed in chapter 7.

Beginning computation

It is not suggested that the beginning of written computational skill must follow the learning of basic number facts — the two areas of learning go hand-in-hand. Number facts to be practised should emerge naturally as recordings of simple operations children have carried out. In an ideal situation, children's written computational skills develop smoothly out of their earlier experiences with recording their practical number operations.

Children usually learn to record addition and subtraction processes on paper in the form of a step-by-step procedure (an algorithm) used to obtain the solution. Children should have no trouble in mastering these procedures if they are linked as closely as possible with the more informal methods of adding and subtracting that are typically used by children before they enter school. Difficulties arise if the processes are taught without reference to children's prior learning or way of recording (Whitebread 1995).

Baroody and Standifer (1993) indicate that most Year 1 students and many kindergarten children can solve straightforward addition problems, using mental calculation, blocks, fingers, pictures or tally marks. It was argued earlier that the transition from concrete understanding to the use of symbolic representation actually has intermediate semi-concrete and semi-abstract stages. This transition can easily be seen in the forms of recording used in the children's workbooks. At a halfway stage toward symbolic representation children may still be using counters, tally marks or dots alongside the simple written calculation. The example below represents both a symbolic and an iconic recording of an operation as they might appear on a child's page.

$$
\begin{array}{rl}
8 & \text{oooooooo} \\
-3 & \text{ooo} \\
\hline
5 & \text{ooooo}
\end{array}
$$

Moving on

An understanding of cardinal value of number, ability in sorting and classifying, counting skills and reversibility of thought are considered necessary for meaningful learning of simple addition and subtraction processes (Sheffield & Cruikshank 1996). Place value is also essential knowledge once children progress to larger numbers.

Gradually, children are introduced to the more conventional use of basic mathematical signs, symbols and notation. Teachers should never make assumptions about the sophistication of children's understanding of even simple signs and symbols. For example, Baroody (1993) makes an interesting point when he reports that some children don't really understand the meaning of the 'equals' sign (=) even though they use it frequently and teachers assume that its meaning is clear. While children may understand that $5 + 3 = 8$ and that $8 = 5 + 3$, they may still not accept that $5 + 3 = 3 + 5$. They may be even less inclined to grasp that $5 + 3 = 4 + 4$. Children may think the sign = means 'makes the answer' rather than 'is the same as'. Lack of certainty about the meaning of other common terms such as 'plus', 'minus', 'difference', 'take away', 'carry', 'borrow', 'rename', 'regroup', 'exchange' and so on has also been identified by Cockburn (1999) as a possible cause of learning failure in early mathematics. Thoroughly teaching the language of the subject is part of effective instruction, and checking for understanding of vocabulary must be given high priority.

Children also need time and practice to understand the complementary and reversible characteristics of addition and subtraction.

$$10 - 2 = 8$$
$$10 - 8 = 2$$
$$8 + 2 = 10$$
$$2 + 8 = 10$$
$$10 = 8 + 2$$
$$10 = 2 + 8$$
$$? + 2 = 10$$
$$10 - ? = 2$$
$$10 \ldots = 8$$

If children have difficulty with the final three examples, an activity can be created in which the unknown number is literally hidden under a small box or card. Children say, 'Something added to 2 makes 10. The something must be …'. (Now they check under the box.) 'Ten take away something leaves 2. The something must be 8.' (Check under the box.) 'Ten, add something or take something, and it leaves 8. It must be take 2', etc.

It is important that children understand the commutative law as early as possible. The commutative law applying to the basic addition and multiplication processes is that the order in which the numbers are presented on one side of the = sign does not affect the sum or product (4 + 3 = 7 and 3 + 4 = 7; 2 x 3 = 6 and 3 x 2 = 6). Later, children need to learn that the commutative principle does not apply to division or to subtraction, where changing the order of the numbers completely changes the problem (17 ÷ 6 is not the same as 6 ÷ 17; nor is 11 − 5 the same as 5 − 11). Although this is perfectly obvious to individuals who have grasped the principle through meaningful recordings of operations, a few children remain utterly confused and tend to, for example, always start any calculation with the smaller number, or some other half-remembered earlier instruction from a different context (Reys et al. 1998).

Interpreting number relationships

Starting with very simple number relationships, children should be encouraged to think about what a 'number sentence' really tells them. In the examples below the intention is to encourage learners to use 'self-questioning' to think rationally about the example, rather than completing it mechanically by rote. Students need a great deal of experience explaining and justifying their answers in both simple and more complex tasks, so that they realise that mathematics is something they are supposed to think about and understand (Baroody 1993; Flood 1999). The teacher's role is to ask questions that invite reflection, explanation, expansion and interpretation, paving the way for a more thoughtful approach to problem-solving (Van de Walle 1998). For example, 'Tell me what you were thinking when you did that'. 'How did your group obtain that answer?' 'Can you show us and tell us how you did that?'

With even the simplest number work, children can be taught to reason and reflect when producing a response. For example:

9 + ? = 12   How could we say that to ourselves?
             'Nine add something makes 12.'
             What must the something be?

15 − ? = 8   How could we say that?
             How could we work out the missing number?
             Show me how you could do that on the number line.
             Say this one to me. ? + 7 + 2 = 13
             Show me how to do that on the number line.

19
− ??
  5   How could we ask ourselves this one?
             Show me that it really is 14.

Number line

The simple number line or number track is one of the most useful aids for making 'visual' the processes of addition (counting on) and subtraction (counting back) (Cockburn 1999). The line can also be used to help with counting in tens, twos, fives and so on. Many children discover the value of a number line for themselves, without formal instruction, and will often be seen using the calibrations on their rulers to count forward or back.

Some structural apparatus, for example Unifix, provides a '1 to 100' number track. The track can be built up over time, starting with a section for 1 to 10 or 1 to 20, and ending with the 1 to 100 when the children are ready for that level of work. With Unifix, the track is designed to accommodate the interlocking cubes so that, for example, a line of cubes assembled to represent 17 can be added to a line of cubes representing 24, to indicate at once that the two together reach 41 on the track. Soon students do not need to use the cubes, but can refer directly to the line in order to carry out the same type of process or to determine, for example, the result of taking 28 from 39.

One interesting thing about the use of cubes and number tracks in the early stages seems to be that children are much less likely to make the error they often make when using their ruler as a number line — counting the lines rather than the intervals and getting the result wrong by one. Using the cubes appears to establish the appropriate visual image of the process.

More will be said later concerning the value of the Unifix Number 1–100 as a method for representing the division process.

From 'number sentences' to algorithms

Exposure to both horizontal and vertical formats for basic addition and subtraction is extremely important. It is natural that horizontal number sentences using pictures, then tallies and finally symbols will have evolved as a recording of actual operations performed with objects. Children will have become proficient and feel comfortable with this mode of recording. For some children, transition from the horizontal to vertical format with number creates a problem unless the two systems for recording and operating are taught together. Adequate time must be spent comparing and relating the two formats. There are indications that certain children abandon logical thinking as soon as they are confronted with a vertical algorithm (Foster 1998). For example, problems they can solve easily in horizontal form are failed when presented vertically.

In the early stages of learning to record addition and subtraction, using tens and units in their horizontal and vertical algorithmic formats, apparatus can be of direct help. The simplest and most relevant materials are bundles of ten small rods (or ice-cream sticks) held together by elastic bands. The operations of 'borrowing' ten, exchanging, grouping and regrouping can be easily represented in semi-concrete terms and related to the appropriate recordings. This approach is beautifully illustrated in the text by Booker et al. (1997).

For example, when 35 is added to 27 using the vertical form of the algorithm, the process can be modelled using three bundles of ten and five single rods in the top position and two bundles of ten and seven single rods in the bottom position. From the five plus seven single rods a new bundle of ten can be made, leaving the two single rods in the units column. The new bundle of ten rods can be placed on the 'model' in the same position as the carrying figure in the written algorithm, thus depicting clearly in visual terms what happens when we 'carry a ten'.

(Reproduced from G. Booker, *Teaching Primary Mathematics*, [2nd edn] with the permission of Pearson Education Australia. Copyright © 1997.)

Language	Materials		Recording
	tens	ones	
Show (record) the two numbers		↓	1
What do you add first? The ones			35
How many ones? 12 ones			+ 27
Are there enough ones to make a ten?			
1 ten 2 ones			2
	tens	ones	
Put the ones with the ones, the 1 ten with the tens		↓	1
What do you add next? The tens			35
How many tens altogether? 6 tens			+ 27
			62
35 and 27 is 62			

Understanding the processes

The notion of 'regrouping' and 'renaming', as in the example above, is vitally important, but not one that children find easy to grasp. The process occurs not only when a new group of ten can be created and moved to the tens column, it also underpins the ability to express a given number in a different form. For example, 87 can be thought of as not just 8 tens and 7 units but as 7 tens and 17 units. Students must understand this to deal with subtraction by the decomposition method. When the subtraction algorithm is mastered purely by rote, students fail to picture mentally what 'borrowing a ten' and 'borrowing a hundred' really mean. This understanding of how numbers can be reconstructed contributes significantly to children's ability to compute mentally and to estimate. Reys et al. (1998, p. 130) rightly comment that, 'The importance of clearly understanding the regrouping process cannot be overstressed. Understanding is most likely to develop when children experience this bridging with physical models and practice trading and regrouping'.

Regular activities and problems which will help students to develop insight into the structure of larger numbers are extremely important. For example, if students are faced with the problem 47 + 17 they could be encouraged to think of it regrouped as:

(40 + 7) + (10 + 7)

The tens are easily combined to make 50, and the two 7s make 14.

50 + 14 = 64

Fewer errors seem to occur with this method than with the 'carrying the bundle of ten to the next column' algorithm. This is almost certainly because the approach encourages students to think rationally about the structure of the numbers being used, rather than apply a procedure by rote (Isaacs & Carroll 1999).

Developing an understanding of the ways in which a number can be reconstructed and translated into other forms, as above, is so very, very important that it is sad to find the concept often relegated to just one small section of a textbook and one week of classroom study and practice. Experience in translating numbers into different forms should be given much more time and attention in mathematics programs. It is part of what constitutes higher-order number sense. Knowing how to conceptualise a number in many different ways is fundamental to understanding most of the procedures children need to use in subtracting, multiplying and dividing, as will become clear later in this chapter.

Dienes Multibase Arithmetic Blocks (MAB) Base 10 are particularly valuable for clearly representing the relative size value and symbolic place value of thousands (Th), hundreds (H), tens (T) and units (U). Many children lack understanding of the relative size of numbers greater than 100, and the opportunity to construct proportional models of numbers such as 2376 using MAB is a powerful experience. Used in conjunction with a place value table with Th, H, T and U columns, the experience helps build a mental (visual) image of what the problem 2376 – 1995 might look like in concrete terms. Baroody (1993) recommends using the written recording directly alongside the concrete representation.

Non-proportional aids, such as an abacus, are less helpful for students with learning difficulties when carrying out addition and subtraction. Making a single bead represent a unit on one row but a ten on the next row, is simply too confusing for lower-ability students to understand.

Place value

Payne and Huinker (1993) insist that there must be a substantial increase in the amount of instructional time devoted to teaching place value. An understanding of place value is absolutely fundamental to meaningful operations with numbers above ten. Mastery of the place value concept takes much longer than many teachers realise (Cockburn 1999). Many activities and experiences involving concrete and visual materials should be used to depict in various ways the idea that, in a base 10 system, quantities in each column increase ten-fold as we move left. For example, the number 4361 is 4000 + 300 + 60 + 1, and the value of the '3' is actually greater than the value of the '6' in the sequence 4361. Baroody

(1993) concludes that research supports the use of manipulative aids to significantly improve students' meaningful learning of base 10 place value concepts and multi-digit algorithms.

Failure to understand how large numbers are constructed can be the point at which meaningful learning gives way to rote learning. The students don't really understand what they are doing, even though application of the right 'trick' at an instrumental level may produce the 'right' answer. A purely algorithmic approach to computation frequently undermines children's construction of meaning, or results in incomplete understanding. Students are forced for the first time to resort to rote learning.

In general, too little time is devoted to concrete work on place value, partly because teachers find it much easier to teach only the procedural knowledge that can quickly result in mechanical completion of a given algorithm than to spend time providing the first-hand experience that leads to conceptual knowledge of the operation. Ma (1999) also suggests that teachers' own understanding may often be limited to a procedural level, causing them to teach only what they themselves know.

Exploring larger numbers

There are at least three ways of approaching addition and subtraction with multi-digit numbers (Baroody & Standifer 1993). These can be summarised briefly as 'discovery', 'teacher-directed' and 'guided discovery'. The teacher-directed approach is didactic and structured, while the other two approaches make greater use of inductive teaching and learning principles.

The 'discovery' approach is one in which children are challenged to find out for themselves ways of solving problems involving large numbers. It is argued that this approach encourages students to investigate and experiment with complex numbers, and thus paves the way for greater confidence, autonomy and initiative in problem-solving. The approach enables children to invent, share and discuss their own ways of dealing with large numbers, based on their prior experience. This investigative approach is excellent for students who are already confident in mathematics and have a good basic number sense; but it may be a frustrating method for children who have learning problems. They are more likely to feel successful if taught effective ways of approaching problems involving large numbers, then given the opportunity to practise and generalise the procedures to other examples. The investigative method can also consume fairly large amounts of class time. Perhaps it is pertinent to point out that Galton et al. (1999) suggest that discovery or enquiry approaches are often difficult to implement in the average classroom due to time constraints, with many other areas of the curriculum competing for available time.

The second approach is teacher-directed and highly structured. The teacher clearly demonstrates the effective way to apply an appropriate algorithm, for example to subtract 877 from 4541. The children may be given MAB or other equipment to represent the numbers, and the teacher will help them to interpret and record each step in the written algorithm. The process is not rote-learning since the logical actions the children are performing with the materials are being talked about and recorded at the same time, under the close direction of the teacher. It is quite unlike the situation of a teacher simply using chalk-and-talk instruction at the blackboard. The semi-concrete/semi-abstract representation being used is visual, and the instruction is focused on making meaning and on understanding number relationships. For lower-ability students this leads to much less confusion and greater confidence.

The third approach, guided discovery, combines elements of the previous two. The teacher might introduce a MAB 'model' of a subtraction or addition problem, together with a written algorithm. Students discuss how the recording relates to the model. They then practise on other examples to check the validity of their ideas and to master the procedure.

Self-direction when solving algorithms

In the early stages of establishing the procedures involved in a specific algorithm, not only must the process be understood, but beginners usually need to talk themselves through it. For example, using the decomposition method for the following subtraction problem, students should verbalise the steps in something similar to the following sequence.

$$581$$
$$- 139$$

Students say:

> Start with the units. I can't take 9 from 1 so I must borrow a ten and write it next to the 1. Now I can call it 11.
> Cross out the 8 tens and write 7 tens.
> Now I can take 9 from 11 and write 2 in the answer under the units column.
> Move to the tens column. 7 tens take 3 tens leaves 4 tens in the answer.
> 5 hundred take 1 hundred leaves 4 in the hundreds column.
> My answer is four hundred and forty-two.

Obviously, students can also check that the answer is correct by adding the 442 to the 139.

Students with learning difficulties, who often lack complete understanding of the algorithm through lack of concrete experience, are easily confused if the 'verbal cueing' used in the classroom is not the same as the cueing used when someone else helps them. Parents may try to assist at home, but may have been taught (by rote) a different procedure. When they try to teach their version the learner's confusion is increased. Even support teachers who attempt to help students with computational processes must liaise closely with the mathematics teacher to find out the precise verbal self-instructions students are expected to use.

Multiplication and division: general points

Unfortunately, in many classrooms teaching multiplication and division processes often occurs after the use of structural material and visual aids has been phased out. This failure to use concrete demonstrations may be partly related to the children's age by the time they are ready to learn intermediate and higher-level multiplication and division. It is felt that they are 'too old' to need apparatus, because that is needed only for very young children. In this context it is important to recall the earlier discussion (see chapter 2) concerning Piaget's somewhat discredited idea that by age twelve most students can operate at an abstract level of reasoning. It is now accepted that concrete and visual representation is still needed into adolescence, particularly if lower-ability students are to develop a conceptual understanding of the processes of multiplication and division with large numbers. In the typical rush to get children to a stage of abstract symbol manipulation, mathematics instruction often moves them rapidly through only a procedural understanding of multiplication and division (Kouba & Franklin 1993). As a result, many children lack real conceptual understanding of the two operations.

Teachers should spend more time helping children explore the processes of multiplication and division, and the reciprocal relationship between the two. It is even important to make sure that students understand that, unlike addition and multiplication, division does not follow the commutative principle. The order in which the numbers occur cannot be reversed: 15 ÷ 5 is not the same as 5 ÷ 15, even though 15 x 5 produces the same result as 5 x 15.

Children need help early in learning multiplication to recognise that division should be thought of as the reverse of the process of multiplication.

Twelve lots of three make thirty-six, so we could make twelve groups of 3 out of thirty-six.
Three children have 12 crayons each. They have 36 crayons altogether. 3 x 12 = 36 crayons.
How many crayons could three children each have if 36 are shared equally among them? 36 ÷ 3 = 12 crayons each.
How many pencils could 12 children have if 36 pencils are shared equally among them? 36 ÷ 12 = 3 pencils each.

Booker et al. (1997, p. 220) observe that, 'Division relies fundamentally on a good understanding of multiplication, both in the form of visualising the initial concept and in the use of multiplication facts to provide answers for the steps involved in the formal procedure'. Too often the two processes have been taught separately, particularly if they occur as different chapters in a textbook. Skemp (1989b), in *Structured activities for primary mathematics*, illustrates how experiences in combining equal groups of objects can be linked with reciprocal experiences in partitioning and sharing those objects. The text by Booker et al. (1997), *Teaching primary mathematics*, also contains excellent material, clearly illustrated to facilitate the teaching of multiplication and division.

The language associated with multiplication and division needs careful attention. Teachers easily assume that children either already know or will quickly pick up terms such as 'factor', 'product', 'multiplied' and 'times'. For example, in the mathematical sentence 4 x 5 = 20, the 4 and the 5 are termed 'factors' and the 20 represents the 'product' of these two factors. The first factor (4) tells us the number of groups or sets, and the second factor identifies how many items in each set (5).

Many of the errors that children make in their arithmetic (e.g. Ashlock 1998; Palmer et al. 1994) can be traced back to evidence that they simply have no idea what the steps in the process really involve. The solution is to take instruction back to a realistic level, using visual material and contexts that children can understand. Unfortunately, the diagnostic procedure commonly associated with error analysis in students' written work often simply results in re-teaching the particular missing 'trick' in the procedure, rather than teaching for insight. An exception to this general rule is the approach suggested by Palmer et al. (1994) in the diagnostic and remedial resource material called *Stop! look and lesson*.

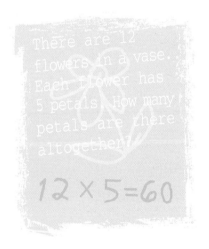

For practical teaching purposes it is very important to ensure that students have sufficient concrete experience with multiplying and dividing in various forms. They need to develop an understanding of the processes involved in the typical algorithms used for calculation. Long multiplication and long division, set down on paper, are all too frequently meaningless for many students, although they may eventually learn by rote the 'tricks' that produce a tick in their exercise books. Serna and Patton (1997) state that the way in which these processes of multiplication and division are commonly taught to students with learning difficulties makes it virtually impossible for them to see connections with real life, and therefore they are unable to apply the skills for any useful purpose outside the context of mathematics lessons.

Specific points on multiplication

There are several main formats for multiplication. The two best-known and most widely used are repeated addition and array multiplication.

Repeated addition

Repeated addition is the situation where a learner writes 17 + 17 + 17 + 17 = ? (or the same in vertical format) and adds, rather than calculating 17 x 4 = ?

Souviney (1994) points out that simple multiplication facts are actually memorised sums from repeated addition exercises: 'six groups of six make thirty-six', 'seven groups of six make forty-two', etc. The use of structural apparatus or counters to build a representation of multiplication tables also depicts a repeated addition model.

```
ooooooo   ooooooo   ooooooo   ooooooo   ooooooo
   7         7         7         7         7         = 35
```

The basis for repeated addition comes from children's increasing familiarity with counting in groups, 'five, ten, fifteen …' or 'four, eight, twelve, sixteen …'. Heddens and Speer (1995) point out that the repeated addition method is not actually multiplication in the algorithmic sense, but it is a model to help children understand the concept of multiplying. The repeated addition method appears to be the one that students with learning difficulties cling to, long after most other students have progressed to algorithmic or mental strategies to complete the same processes.

Array multiplication

This refers to the understanding that the multiplication of two numbers can be represented or visualised as a rectangle, the column representing the number of items in one set and the rows representing the number of such sets. Using squared paper will provide the required visual representation, but it is also possible to build up multiplication rectangles using structural apparatus such as the hundreds, tens and unit blocks from MAB.

Reminding students of their earlier understanding of how numbers can be regrouped or expanded and translated into different forms, together with a thorough understanding of place value, may help them understand what is occurring at each stage in the following multiplication algorithm. It is not suggested that this is the easiest or quickest way to record this algorithm, but the items in brackets on the right help students to think about what each of the four steps in a TU x TU multiplication actually involves.

```
       56
     x 23
       18  (3 x 6)
      150  (3 x 50)
      120  (20 x 6)
     1000  (20 x 50)
     1288
```

The traditional algorithm for long multiplication (e.g. 64 x 32) usually looks something like the example below.

```
64 x 32 = ?
       64
     x 32
      128
     1920
     2048
```

The process may be better appreciated by learners in the early stages if the two steps in the calculation are carried out and recorded separately, before being combined (Daly & Buruma 1997).

64 x 32 = ?

(i)   32 can be thought of as 30 + 2

(ii) Multiply first by the units (ones)

```
         64
       x  2
        128
```

(iii) Multiply next by the tens

```
         64
       x 30
       1920
```

(iv) Altogether 64 x 32 = 2048 (128 + 1920)

Specific points on division

This book stresses that division and multiplication are best taught in tandem, rather than sequentially. There are times, however, particularly in remedial teaching situations, where specific focus needs to be given to the division processes.

Children are reported to have more difficulty with division than with any other operation (Galton et al. 1999; Reynolds & Farrell 1996). This seems to stem mainly from the fact that even the simplest level of division is taught as an abstract process through chalk-and-talk. Blackboard examples of the algorithm are used without referring to real objects or to children's natural experiences with sorting, grouping and sharing. The process of partitioning and sharing are decontextualised, and the steps of the algorithm are not understood. Children lose sight of what the process has really involved. Heddens and Speer (1995, p. 128) are absolutely correct when they state:

> The understanding of division has often been neglected, because so much emphasis has been placed on memorising the algorithm and developing the skill of computation. Also research tells us that division is the most difficult algorithm to teach, although it is not the most difficult operation to understand.

Making division 'visual' is important. Students need to see what happens when larger groups are subdivided and shared, and what it really means to have a 'remainder'. The principle of multiple embodiment (Dienes 1963) can be applied here by finding as many everyday examples as possible of quantities being divided for real purposes. For example, the Unifix Number 1–100 can be used to provide a very clear embodiment of the division process in semi-concrete form. A line of 38 cubes in the track can have a 'division marker' inserted between, say, every sixth cube, thus modelling very clearly that when 38 is divided or partitioned in this way it will form six groups of six with two blocks 'left over' (a visual indication of what we mean by 'remainder').

It is important for students to experience division problems stated in different ways. For example, a problem might be, 'If 50 video-discs are separated into five equal sets, how many video-discs will be in each set?' This asks how many there are in each set. Another problem might ask, 'If 50 video-discs are divided into boxes of 10, how many boxes will there be?' This asks how many boxes (sets) there will be. Children need to discuss the ways in which these two problems require a different format for written recording ($50 \div 5 = ?$ and $50 \div 10 = ?$).

Reys et al. (1998) compare the 'distributive algorithm' for division with the 'subtractive algorithm'. Usually, schools teach only the distributive method, as in the example below.

```
        97 r1
    4 ) 389    How many 4s in 38? (9 x 4 = 36)
        36
        29     How many 4s in 29? (7 x 4 = 28)
        28
        r1
```

The subtractive approach encourages students to take out any easily divisible number recognised within the number to be divided, deal with it, then find the next easy number to divide, and so on. Finally the quotients from each smaller division are totalled and any remainder recorded. For example, $389 \div 4$.

```
4 ) 389
     200     I know that 200 can easily be divided by 4 (50 x 4)
     189
     160     I know that 160 can be divided easily by 4 (40 x 4)
      29
      28     I know that 28 can be easily divided by 4 (7 x 4)
       1 (remainder)          Solution: 50 + 40 + 7 = 97 r1
```

It can be argued that in this example the procedure requires students to think carefully about the actual size of the dividend, rather than applying a rote-learned script that requires them to say, '4 into 3 won't go. 4 into 38 …'. Given that the '38' here is actually 380, students lose sight of what the division of a group of 389 into 4 smaller groups really involves.

In the multiplication and division examples, alternative algorithmic ways of dealing with the problems have been presented. Those that are more detailed and that focus on understanding each step in the process may be regarded as temporary strategies. In the long term, students would be expected to adopt the quickest and most efficient procedure for carrying out the process — including the use of a calculator.

Using a calculator

While stressing the importance of teaching computational skills with understanding to all students, there is still a valid argument that says time spent on mastering arithmetic procedures and algorithms is largely wasted for students who cannot seem to retain the steps involved in carrying out particular procedures, no matter how much practice they have. Using a calculator as a permanent alternative is totally defensible in such cases (Clark 1999; Drosdeck 1995).

For many students with serious learning problems, teaching the appropriate steps for multiplication and division on a calculator will often be more functional than hours spent on paper-and-pencil procedural drill. The time saved can be better spent establishing an understanding of the actual operations of multiplying and dividing, and recognising when they are needed.

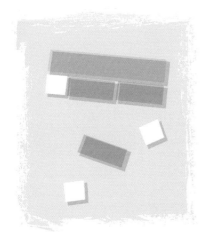

The use of a calculator removes a major obstacle for students with poor computational skills, and they can all compute with speed and accuracy. The instructional time saved can then be devoted to helping the students learn the correct strategies needed to solve problems, rather than spending time and effort on the lower-level cognitive demands of the task. The result is more time available for problem-solving, not less. Research indicates that the use of calculators does not result in overall poorer mental number skills in children (Silver 1997).

Number skills must be functional

Knowing how to compute is a very important skill, but it is of little value if students cannot apply the skill in everyday life and use it for real purposes (Grant 1998). Boaler (1997) suggests that when mathematics is taught badly, students are not encouraged to think about the procedures and rules they are taught to use. They begin to believe that mathematical learning is only about remembering facts and processes, and passing tests. They do not see school mathematics as having anything to do with real life. What they learn, often mainly by rote, remains inert knowledge, of no value once they have passed an examination or benchmark and moved on to new things.

Herman (1994) makes the important point that a balanced approach to mathematics learning and teaching requires both competence in computational skills and a conceptual understanding. It also requires constant application to problem-solving and quantitative investigation, discussed more fully in chapter 5.

> Using mathematics in almost any real context involves being able to choose what mathematical skills to apply from clues of varying strengths. A curriculum that emphasises the real life uses of mathematics must develop this ability (Stacey 1997, p. 72).

5 Teaching problem-solving skills and strategies

For children to develop successful problem-solving techniques, instruction must begin early and be constantly nurtured as each new mathematical concept is introduced and developed (Heddens & Speer 1995, p. 46).

In previous chapters we have seen that the focus of instruction in mathematics has moved increasingly toward developing skills and strategies needed for solving problems, rather than emphasising the rote memorisation of computational tricks and procedures. In the past an algorithmic approach to mathematics education had become an end in itself, with 'numeracy' being interpreted rather narrowly as competence in basic arithmetic. The current concept of numeracy is much broader. It embraces knowing how, when and where to apply number skills for everyday functional purposes (Steen 1999).

It is sometimes assumed that young children, and children with learning difficulties, need to acquire a sound foundation of arithmetic skills before they can begin to engage in any 'real' problem-solving. This is not the case, and such a restricted view can lead to the situation where number skills are taught without children understanding their real meaning. In an ideal situation, simple but interesting problem-solving activities should provide part of the context in which even kindergarten children can acquire new concepts and develop their number skills. The complexity of the problems obviously needs to be age-appropriate and the methods and resources used must reflect the children's developmental level; but the principle of learning about (and through) problem-solving in context applies at all ages and for all ability levels (Hembree & Marsh 1993). Instead of being seen as something that children 'move on to' after they have mastered arithmetic, appropriate problems should provide an interesting and motivating way for new concepts and skills to be acquired, as well as an opportunity for applying and practising existing skills.

In the US, the National Council of Teachers of Mathematics (1989) recommends that problem-solving not be seen as a distinct topic to be taught in isolation, but as the central theme that permeates the entire number and mathematics program at all age levels. This is not to suggest that every mathematics lesson must be devoted entirely to solving new problems. It is acknowledged that time must also be devoted to practice and the consolidation of core skills. The emphasis on problem-solving simply indicates that mathematics should be presented chiefly through meaningful and relevant contexts. The same message is implicit in the *National statement on mathematics for Australian schools* (Australian Education Council 1991).

Reys et al. (1998, p. 69) regard problem-solving not so much as a subsection of the mathematics curriculum as 'a way of teaching'. Working with problems provides one way to help students engage in interesting and challenging learning. This suggests a very different situation from the one described by Frobisher (1994), where traditional mathematical problems set in school frequently fail to interest or appeal to students because the problems are merely boring exercises contrived to allow some previously taught process or strategy to be applied and practised. Such exercises lack relevance, interest and excitement.

What are 'problems'?

Booker et al. (1997, p. 32) define a problem as 'a task for which there is no immediate or obvious solution'. The process of obtaining a solution involves some degree of exploration, analysis and discovery. It may also involve a degree of trial and error. Similarly, Broomes and Petty (1995) indicate that solving a problem necessitates deliberate searching for appropriate action in order to attain an outcome not immediately obvious to the student.

Steen (1999) differentiates between two types of problem, those that are 'standard' or routine, and those that are 'non-routine'. Routine problems, often referred to as 'word problems', can usually be solved by the straightforward application of previously mastered strategies or procedures. A simple example is, 'Mrs Jackson's fourteen hens each lay one egg per day. How many eggs will Mrs Jackson collect from them over a period of three weeks?'

Non-routine problems are unusual and perplexing problems that may not have been encountered before and therefore demand original thinking. This is the part of mathematics that does not rely so much on remembering number facts and procedures as on reasoning ability (Usnick & McCoy 1995). All problem-solving relies to some extent upon recall of relevant information and previously taught skills; but non-routine problems also demand a novel and creative use of strategies. Coffland and Cuevas (1992) indicate that the features that identify a problem as non-routine are:

- there are no readily available steps for the solution;
- creative thought is required;
- previous knowledge, experience and insight will have to be synthesised and applied to a new context.

An example of a non-routine problem is, 'In our classroom we are going to make a 4-minute timer, using a big glass funnel, a tall jar and some fine-grain sand. How will we mark the jar so that we can measure 1 minute, 2 minutes,

3 minutes and 4 minutes with our timer? If we change the sand from fine grain to coarse grain, will the times we have marked on the jar still be accurate? If not, does this mean that more of the coarse sand or less of the coarse sand runs through the funnel in each minute?'

Students need experience with both routine and non-routine problems in order to gain confidence and acquire a repertoire of strategies for tackling the unfamiliar. We might refer to this as developing an individual's 'problem-solving schema'.

Coffland and Cuevas (1992) suggest that although students do not have to master a large number of routine problems before meeting non-routine problems, working with routine problems first can be useful in helping to build both problem-solving abilities and confidence. For most learners, particularly students with learning problems, the simple strategies acquired from successfully solving routine problems create a sound base from which to attempt non-routine and more challenging problems.

How do we solve problems?

Although described differently by different writers, it is generally accepted that there are recognisable and teachable stages through which an individual passes when solving problems. These stages can be summarised as:

- identification of the problem to be solved;
- interpretation of processes and steps needed;
- translation of the information into an appropriate algorithm (or sequence of algorithms);
- calculation;
- evaluation of the result.

In addition to the cognitive skills involved in these five stages there are significant metacognitive components (Sternberg 1999). These components include the self-monitoring and self-correcting questions learners need to use when approaching a problem. For example:

- 'What needs to be worked out in this problem?' (identify the problem);
- 'How will I try to do this?' (select or create a strategy);
- 'Can I picture this problem in my mind?' (visualise);
- 'Is this working out OK?' (self-monitoring);
- 'How will I check if my solution is correct?' (evaluation);
- 'I need to correct this error and then try again' (self-correction).

Solving a problem is not always as easy as simply applying a pretaught algorithm. Non-routine problems need to be analysed, explored for possible actions to take and procedures to use, and then the result checked.

Wilson, Fernandez and Hadaway (1993) comment that traditional models of teaching problem-solving were limited because they always presented problem-solving as a linear task, involving specific steps to be taken in sequence. The approach also implied that a set procedure for solving all problems could be memorised and applied to any problem.

It is evident that in effective problem-solving the process is cyclic, not linear (Booker et al. 1997; Wilson, Fernandez & Hadaway 1993). Each step in solving a problem efficiently requires a metacognitive (self-monitoring) 'checking and looking back' component. This self-checking is thought to help not only with final appraisal of the appropriateness of the answer for a particular problem, it also helps learners reflect upon the general effectiveness of the procedure they have used. Wilson, Fernandez and Hadaway (1993) admit, however, that getting students to look back and reflect on strategies is very difficult indeed. Students with learning difficulties in particular tend not to reflect upon the way they have obtained a solution; they simply want someone else to tell them whether the answer is 'right' or 'wrong'.

Teaching problem-solving approaches

Many students with learning difficulties appear confused when faced with a problem to be solved. They may have difficulty in reading the words or comprehending the meaning of specific terms (McIntosh 1997; Xin & Jitendra 1999). They may have difficulty in sifting the information and selecting appropriate procedures to use. This is particularly the case if the problem context is unfamiliar to them or the problem involves very large numbers. It is as if they cannot relate these large numbers to common-sense processes they use confidently every day to deal with smaller amounts in similar contexts (Enright & Choate 1997). Their recall of basic number facts may also be very slow and inaccurate. This slowness reduces the number of problems they can complete in the lesson, and thus results in less practice for the very students who need it most. Finally, they may fail to generalise and transfer a successful problem-solving strategy to another situation simply because they have acquired an understanding of the strategy only at an instrumental rather than a relational level.

Most students with learning difficulties need to be taught how to approach a problem without feelings of panic or hopelessness. They must be taught effective ways of approaching any problem. Salend (1994), for example, suggests that they be taught how to sift relevant from irrelevant information, how to identify exactly what the problem requires and how to determine the best way of obtaining and checking the result. In other words, they need to be taught the very things that other students who are efficient and confident problem-solvers already know and do. To achieve this, direct teaching at an early stage is necessary for greater independence later. Direct teaching of this type has a proven record of success (Swanson 1999; Tarver 1996). Given that a 'cognitive strategy' can be thought of as a mental plan of action which enables an individual to approach a task in a reasonably systematic manner, and at the same time to monitor the effectiveness of that strategy, it is obvious that students need to be taught such 'plans of action' to tackle mathematics problems.

Much of what we already know about effective teaching (Harris 1999) has an important place. In particular, the teacher needs to:

- model and demonstrate effective strategies for solving routine and non-routine problems;
- 'think aloud' as various aspects of the problem are analysed and possible procedures for solution identified;
- reflect upon the effectiveness of the procedure used.

Once students have been exposed to an effective strategy they have the opportunity to apply it themselves under teacher guidance with feedback, and are finally able to use the strategy independently and generalise it to other problem contexts. The sequence for teaching problem-solving to students with learning difficulties therefore follows a sequence from teacher-direction to final student-centred control (Van de Walle 1998).

The original approaches to strategy training provided some promising results but, as Booker et al. (1997) point out, most of the situations in which the strategies were taught were contrived, and students were not very successful in using the strategies in any generalised way. Encouraging children to try different approaches, rather than drilling one specific way, is likely to help them become more adaptable and flexible in their approach to mathematics problems.

Teaching problem-solving is not an easy task for the teacher, and to improve in this area takes time (Van de Walle 1998). Some authorities (e.g. Galton et al. 1999) even suggest that the reason some countries have students who are better at pure arithmetic than they are at solving problems is because too little time is available in school to develop this type of conceptual learning.

Collaborative group work

If all students are to develop problem-solving skills, they must have time for discussing, comparing and reflecting on their various methods of solution with other individuals (peers and adults). The metacognitive aspects of self-monitoring and self-correction need to be included. Mevarech (1999) encourages teachers to use metacognitive training within cooperative group work, to enable students to analyse, focus on relevant information, share ideas on ways of approaching a problem and reflect on results. Mevarech comments, however, that simply setting up collaborative group work is not enough to enhance students' mathematical thinking. A structure must be imposed on the discussion that reflects the components listed below. Group discussion can be based on a framework such as:

- 'What is involved in this problem?' (orientation and comprehension);
- 'Is this problem similar to any other problem we have tackled?' (comparison);
- 'What approach do we need to take to solve this?' (strategy selection);
- 'How is this method working out?' (monitoring);
- 'Does our result make sense?' (evaluation).

Because discussion and collaboration are so valuable in developing and enhancing problem-solving strategies, classroom approaches such as 'reciprocal teaching' are useful (Brown & Palincsar 1989; Rosenshine & Meister 1994). Reciprocal teaching is an approach used more often in teaching reading comprehension skills and study skills in the language arts area, but has much to offer in the development of mathematical problem-solving skills. In reciprocal teaching the teacher and students take it in turns to lead discussion and raise questions about a specific text (in this case, a word problem in maths). The teacher models, through thinking aloud, task-appropriate processes such as clarifying, identifying key information, predicting, planning an approach, attempting a solution and reflecting on the outcome (Sabornie & deBettencourt 1997). Students participate at whatever level they can, with the teacher providing guidance and feedback. The students take turns as discussion leader and guide their peers through the activities, focusing on making meaning and collaborating on ways of approaching the task.

Problem-solving and learning difficulties

Sabornie and deBettencourt (1997), Swanson (1999) and Xin and Jitendra (1999) review the results from a number of intervention studies designed to improve the problem-solving ability of learning-disabled students. They conclude that it is possible to improve this area of performance using, for example, many of the strategies and techniques described below. Their analysis of the research also indicates that longer-term interventions are much more effective than short-term ones, and that students must gain better independent control of the strategies if there is to be any likelihood of them being able to generalise the strategy. Gaining such self-control requires the students to reason and reflect on the procedures they use, not merely carry out in rote style the procedures directly taught by others. It is said that students who learn to monitor and regulate their own problem-solving behaviours show improvement in problem-solving (Van de Walle 1998, p. 51).

Specific strategies

Basically all the strategies focus on helping students become more confident and independent in identifying what the problem is asking, selecting appropriate procedures to use, self-monitoring while attempting the solution, and checking the reasonableness of the result obtained. There are a number of common strategies for solving both routine and non-routine problems.

Use a model or concrete materials

Examples

Using Cuisenaire rods, begin with the yellow rod and add three white rods to one end. Which rod exactly equals the line you have made?
If the value of the yellow rod is 5, write the number sentence to record what you have just discovered.

How many sticky labels exactly the size of a 45c postage stamp will be needed to completely cover the surface of a piece of card 15 cm x 12 cm?

For students not yet at an abstract level of thinking and reasoning, this type of problem-solving approach is essential. Clayton (1999) advocates providing materials (manipulatives) together with careful guidance in how they can be used to model the problem. Useful experience can be gained through getting children to translate problems into simple number sentences (mathematical statements) then representing these in concrete terms, and vice versa.

Make a drawing or diagram

Example

The city of Trantville is exactly 200 km north of Butan. Butan is 90 km due east of Seatown. Approximately how far is Trantville from Seatown?

Sternberg (1999) suggests that differences in students' ability to represent problems mentally can mean the difference between success and failure in mathematics. Studies show that teaching children how to use drawings and diagrams to represent problem situations has been extremely helpful in developing their ability to solve the problem (Hembree & Marsh 1993; Kelly 1999). It is argued that the diagrams provide an intermediate stage of representation, helping to bridge students' understanding from the semi-concrete level to more abstract use of symbols. Herr and Johnson (1994, p. 9) comment that, 'Much problem-solving revolves around information and how it is organised. When you draw a diagram, you organise the information in a spatial manner, which then allows the visual part of your brain to become involved in the problem-solving process'.

Dawe (1993) states that the human mind has the capacity to form mental images which can then be utilised for many different purposes. The use of drawings and diagrams is directly linked to the importance of making mathematics more visual. One of the ways in which children can be encouraged to make greater use of visual images is through the teacher making explicit use of visual aids, pictures and diagrams in teaching mathematics. Children can be encouraged to make greater use of visualisation, and this may help them to process information more efficiently in working memory (Ostoja 1997).

As children do not automatically use the strategy of drawing or making a diagram, encouraging them to do so requires explicit instruction, teacher demonstration, and practice. Simply asking children to draw a picture to represent a problem may not be sufficient. It is the discussion and questioning that can be focused on the picture that will help students make connections and grasp the relationships (Xin & Jitendra 1999).

Act it out

Example

Debra is giving out free cinema tickets to a number of people who buy a book from the bookstall. She begins by giving the first person ten free tickets, the second person nine free tickets, the third person eight free tickets and so on, until all the tickets are gone. How many tickets does she have, and to how many people can she give tickets in this way?

This act-it-out (solving by doing) strategy is helpful mainly for young children or for those who are developmentally delayed. Acting out a problem using real or substitute objects helps to place the problem at a very real and concrete level. Examples of shopping activities, with buying and giving change, are solved best in the early stages by acting them out.

Removing irrelevant detail from the problem

Example

A new book by young author Kit Byers (age 19) sold 8320 copies in Australia this year. The author gets paid 10% of the sale price of each book. The book costs $28. On how much gross income will the publisher have to base the 10% payment to the author?

Students should be encouraged to underline only the relevant detail needed to answer the question. This strategy is particularly useful for students with reading comprehension difficulties, and for those who wrongly assume that they have to use every number that appears in the problem when obtaining a solution.

Construct a table and / or graph

Example

The students in Meng's class carry out a count of the traffic passing their school gate over a 30-minute period starting at 9 a.m. They count each type of vehicle separately. One child counts cars (58). Another counts buses (17). Other students count vans (27), trucks (30), motorcycles (20) and bicycles (8). They repeat the count for another 30-minute period starting at 2 p.m. and record cars (24), buses (5), vans (12), trucks (32), motorcycles (8) and bicycles (1). How could the students show the results of their traffic survey? What conclusions could they draw from it?

Some very useful practical examples of drawing, charting and tabulating are provided in the text by Kennedy and Tipps (1994). Basically, this strategy helps with the organisation of relevant information and at the same time makes relationships between the various components of the task more visual.

Guess, try then check

Example

Susan went to a toyshop with the money she had been given for her birthday. She spent exactly $20. What did she probably buy from this list?
Painting set $12.60
Doll $4.50
Robot $7.65
Construction kit $24
Stamp album $7.40
Mask $5.50

It is often suggested that this is the most commonly used strategy in many everyday mathematics situations. 'Guessing' should not be random, but based on some attempt at estimating and approximating (through such substrategies as rounding-up numbers or rounding-down).

Account for all possibilities

Example

Using Unifix blocks of different colours, how many ways can you build a train nine blocks long? How might you record each train on paper to show how it is different from all the others?

If part of becoming an efficient problem-solver is thinking creatively and reflectively as well as analytically, problems should encourage students not to jump to a conclusion or to seek the easiest answer, but to explore all possibilities. In situations like this brainstorming for ideas can be useful. The teacher's role is to stimulate investigation through appropriate questioning, such as 'That's good. It works out that way. Could we do it a different way too?'

Simplify or break into parts

Example

The price of apartments has been rising at an average rate of 5% per year. If you bought an apartment ten years ago for $88 890, roughly what would it be worth now? If you sold it for $100 000 would you have made a profit or a loss? How much would you have gained or lost?

The context of the problem could be changed to buying a foreign stamp for $10. The stamp value increases 10% per year. The problem is then broken down into steps: 'What is 10% of $10? So what would the stamp be worth after one year? What is 10% of $11? Now let's try the same steps with the apartment problem'. This strategy can be helpful to students who seem overwhelmed with large numbers, or with problems that have more than one step. Usnick and McCoy (1995) suggest the stumbling-block for some students attempting to work problems is the size of the numbers used. They suggest that by first working a similar problem involving exactly the same concepts and processes, but with much smaller numbers, the students focus on what to do and how to do it and can then transfer this understanding to the original problem.

Work backwards

Example

Darren had $15 when he went to the supermarket to buy cheese, fruit and bread. He came away with $1.60 change. He knew that the cheese had cost $5.40 and the fruit $6.20. How much did the bread cost?

The children are taught to ask themselves, 'How much did he have left out of $15? So how much did he spend altogether? How much did the cheese and fruit cost together? So how much did the bread cost?'

It should be noted that some students apply the working-backwards strategy through necessity when confronted with a difficult problem in their textbook or for homework. They look at the answer in the back of the book and think, 'If this is the answer, how do I get that result from these figures in the problem?'

Using variety in problem types

In order to expose students to key aspects of approaching problems and to explicitly discuss the importance of considering specific points, Reys et al. (1998) suggest that teachers should make sure that they often include problems with the following characteristics :

- too much or too little information;
- the need to estimate a result;
- that relate to practical applications in consumer or business contexts;
- that require students to conceptualise very large or very small numbers;
- that require reasoning, conjecture and checking;

- that contain more than one step to reach the solution;
- that have more than one possible answer, according to the interpretation and approach taken.

Acronyms and mnemonics

Several writers have described specific strategies with acronyms and mnemonics to help students remember a strategy and its steps. Examples of such cued strategies include:

- The 'ROSE' strategy (Enright & Choate 1997)

  R = Read the question

  O = Organise the facts

  S = Select the operation and solve

  E = Evaluate the answer.

- The 'SOLVE' strategy (Miller & Mercer 1993)

  S = See the sign

  O = Observe the information and try a solution

  L = Look or draw

  V = Verify your answer

  E = Enter your result.

- 'RAVE CCC' (Westwood 1997)

  R = Read the problem carefully

  A = Attend to any words which may suggest the process to use

  V = Visualise the problem (or draw)

  E = Estimate a possible answer

  C = Choose the appropriate numbers

  C = Calculate

  C = Check your result against your estimate.

Specific needs of students with learning difficulties

In discussing the instructional needs of students with learning difficulties, Enright and Choate (1997) advise that a successful problem-solving program in mathematics should focus on systematically teaching these students a repertoire of strategies for solving problems. All the strategies above, and many others described in the literature, are valuable in this respect.

Enright and Choate indicate that the five main areas where instruction may be needed are:

- reading a problem with understanding;
- sifting and organising the data;

- selecting the appropriate operations;
- carrying out the necessary calculations;
- evaluating the answer.

Additional teaching points to consider when planning to improve the problem-solving abilities of learning-disabled students include:

- preteaching the vocabulary associated with word problems so that comprehension is enhanced;
- providing cues (such as directional arrows) to indicate where to begin calculations and in which direction to proceed;
- using games and other activities to improve automaticity in such things as recall of number facts and recognition of specific symbols and signs;
- linking problems to the students' own life experiences;
- giving children experience in setting their own problems for others to do;
- stressing self-checking and praising self-correction.

In the review of interventions reported by Xin and Jitendra (1999) the following approaches all proved to be effective in improving students' ability to solve problems:

- use of diagramming;
- manipulatives;
- metacognitive training;
- visualising;
- estimating;
- computer-aided instruction (CAI);
- use of a calculator;
- looking for key words.

Their review looked not only at the immediate effect of any intervention but also at evidence that the new learning was being maintained over time and generalised to other contexts. The results suggested that CAI, the use of visual

representations (e.g. drawing a picture or diagram), explicit strategy training and metacognitive training (e.g. teaching the students to self-question and self-instruct using previously taught steps) all proved to be helpful in advancing students' problem-solving skills — students became more self-directed. The authors point out that students respond differently to an intervention, suggesting that prior knowledge and existing skill level influence response. For interventions to be truly effective they need to be based on a careful appraisal of the students' existing knowledge and skills (Westwood 1998).

Teaching primary mathematics by Booker et al. (1997) is particularly useful in helping teachers understand more about the processes involved in solving problems, and gives some excellent examples. Other valuable sources include *Problem-solving strategies: crossing the river with dogs* by Herr and Johnson (1994) and *The new sourcebook for teaching reasoning and problem-solving in elementary school* by Krulik and Rudnick (1995). Van de Walle's (1998) book *Elementary and middle school mathematics: teaching developmentally* presents an extremely well-argued rationale for teaching problem-solving, and provides guidance for teachers' planning based on Polya's (1957) model. A useful text that focuses on students with learning difficulties is *Successful inclusive teaching*, edited by Choate (1997). Chapter 11 in that text provides many examples of interventions that can be used with learning-disabled students.

6 Assessment

Assessment should provide both teacher and students with ongoing feedback concerning progress towards goals. Assessment should provide information concerning more than simple mastery of procedural skills. It should inform each individual student and teacher about growth toward mathematical power and problem-solving ability (Van de Walle 1998, p. 64).

In recent years the teaching of mathematics has generally adopted a more diagnostic approach. This is clear in the comment from Stenmark (1991, p. 5): 'Increasingly we find advantages in blurring the lines between instruction and assessment, in drawing assessment information from instructional tasks, and in providing additional instruction in the context of assessment activities'. In any classroom mathematics program there is a need for regular assessment of individual progress. Accurate assessment of a student's current competencies must be the starting point for any intervention at the individual level. Using such assessment and reporting instruments as *Mathematics: a curriculum profile for Australian schools* (Australian Education Council 1994), together with teacher-made and curriculum-based tests, teachers are able to monitor closely the knowledge, skills and strategies their students possess. The information gained from ongoing assessment can then be used to ensure the essential precision in program planning and adaptation.

Purposes of assessment

Assessment in the curriculum area of numeracy serves the same basic functions as assessment in other areas of the curriculum. These functions include:

- checking on the overall efficacy of the teaching program;
- determining any particular student's stage of development;
- gaining information about students' specific weaknesses and special instructional needs;
- identifying any concepts or procedures which may need to be re-taught or reviewed.

The content of the curriculum, the aims and objectives for the subject and the processes of assessment should be closely linked. It is the regular assessment of students' performance in relation to the set curriculum objectives that informs teachers about the effectiveness of their programs and identifies any potential difficulties for some students (Carter, Frobisher & Roper 1994).

Approaches to assessment

In the numeracy domain, the following procedures are appropriate for obtaining relevant information:

- observation of students engaged in mathematical activities;
- questioning students individually or in small group contexts;
- analysing samples of students' written work;
- applying teacher-made or published tests;
- using a basic inventory or checklist of core knowledge and skills;
- diagnostic testing (which may include any or all of the above).

Each of these approaches to assessment will be discussed in more detail below. It is important to point out that these sources of information about students' knowledge and skill are not mutually exclusive. Particularly in the case of students with learning problems, information from several different sources is almost always required to plan appropriate intervention strategies.

Observing students at work

Among the more dynamic methods of assessing students' learning, direct observation of the ways in which they tackle the tasks set is one of the most natural extensions of the teaching–learning process (Sheffield & Cruikshank 1996). The teacher will know in advance what to look for in terms of understanding and application in each lesson, and direct observation of students at work can provide this evidence.

All students need feedback on how well they are progressing, and for most students this type of ongoing, informal, curriculum-based monitoring of classroom work is sufficient. The teacher obtains a fairly clear picture of which students are progressing well and which require additional follow-up. Assessment through ongoing observation also allows the teacher to praise individuals who are working well and showing initiative in their approach to a task. For example, 'Well done, Cherie. Organising all that information into a table will help you to solve the problem'. 'Great idea to draw those ladders in order of size, Frank. That will help you to compare them.' Supportive comments and clues can also be used to keep other students on-task, or to help them focus on key aspects of the work. Often minor problems with the setting-out of written work in exercise books can be dealt with at the time, rather than later when books are passed in for marking.

Direct observation will provide the teacher with evidence related not only to the cognitive objectives for the lesson but with information on the affective aspects of students' engagement in the work. For example, the teacher will notice if students are interested in and motivated by the tasks, and if they are confident, hesitant or anxious. It will also be evident whether students are monitoring their own performance and self-correcting where necessary. For example, classroom observation will provide an opportunity to see what action students take to help themselves when they are not sure what to do. Observation of students at work will reveal any difficulties certain students have in keeping on-task.

Reys et al. (1998) advocate that teachers keep reasonably detailed records of what they have observed during lessons, particularly where the evidence suggests that something may need to be taught again or that additional practice or different examples may be required. Booker et al. (1997) provide very useful examples of concise record-keeping at individual student and whole-class levels.

While direct observation is done most easily when students are engaged in routine activities or exercises designed to practise and consolidate previously taught knowledge or skills, it should also be done when the teacher attempts to assess the students' problem-solving strategies (Enright & Choate 1997). The current emphasis on collaborative group work for problem-solving gives the teacher the opportunity to listen to students' discussions and explanations. In the group context, the teacher can also use questions to probe for depth of understanding, or to request that specific students provide an overview or summary of the conclusions the group has reached. Where the teacher suspects that a student has not understood some aspect of the problem or has not yet mastered that type of problem-solving strategy, the teacher can then work more closely with that student for more in-depth assessment and re-teaching (Van den Heuvel-Panhuizen 1996).

Individual assessment and interviews

Situations in which individual assessment occur include:

- for diagnostic purposes, when a student is observed to be having difficulty with the current topic of study;
- when a new student joins the school and the teacher needs to obtain a fairly clear picture of their knowledge and abilities;
- when an educational psychologist or counsellor carries out an appraisal of mathematical skills as part of an overall assessment of a student's abilities and aptitudes.

Some authorities (e.g. Stenmark 1991) see individual interviews as something that should occur periodically with all students, in much the same way that teachers and students confer over written work in the language arts domain. Reys et al. (1998, p. 55) describe an individual interview with a student as a 'powerful way to learn about a student's thinking and to give him or her some special attention'. It is not, of course, necessary to spend equal amounts of time on individual assessment with every student. The way in which teachers identify the students who require more or less time for consultation is an example of instructional differentiation in action. While an individual interview may be designed to monitor a particular student's overall understanding of the current area of study, it is more likely to be done for diagnostic purposes when a student is having difficulties.

Assessing problem-solving skills

When assessing problem-solving skills in individual students, the information presented in chapter 5 provides the appropriate framework . For example, if students are having difficulties with routine problems the teacher may need to check:

- Can they actually read the problem in terms of recognising and decoding the words?
- Having read the words, do they understand what they have read or are there any difficulties with vocabulary (word meanings)?
- Are they able to explain the problem?
- Can they identify the appropriate process to apply?
- Are they able to encode the correct algorithm?
- Can they complete the algorithm correctly, swiftly and confidently?
- Do they appear to have difficulty in recalling basic number facts?
- Are they able to check the reasonableness of the result they obtain?
- Do they self-correct when necessary?

Most of the questions above also apply to non-routine problems but extra attention must be given also to the following issues:

- Do they have any way of starting the problem?
- Can they identify the relevant information presented in the problem?
- Can they explain a strategy they think might help in this problem?
- Do they benefit from any clue or hint the teacher might provide?
- Do they spontaneously make use of resources or aids (e.g. manipulatives, number line, tally marks, drawing a picture, using a calculator)?
- What do they do if their first attempt is unsuccessful?
- How long are they willing to persevere with the problem?

In the case of both routine and non-routine problems it is important to observe whether students tend to make careless errors through inaccurate encoding or untidy placement of the algorithm on the page. Some students with learning difficulties will require special attention to help them become more systematic and careful in their bookwork. In some cases, pages may have to be prepared with cueing marks to show where to begin the calculation and how to align numerals in columns. Exercise books with clearly marked quarter-inch squares are very helpful to many students.

The interview procedure devised by Newman (1983) enables teachers or educational psychologists to analyse the types of difficulty a student may be having with various problems. Her analysis allows for identification of reading difficulties (decoding and comprehension), translation of a problem into an appropriate arithmetic process, and accuracy in encoding and working through the process (algorithm). The student's level of motivation, and any tendency toward carelessness, are also appraised.

Work samples

Work samples can provide the basis for individual interviews with students. Specific problems can be the focus of in-depth analysis of what the student does and does not understand (Booker 1999; Howell, Fox & Morehead 1993). From the teacher's point of view, the focus of an individual assessment is often the student's exercise book or other work sample, or the results of a teacher-made, curriculum-based test. Through direct questioning, and asking the student to explain or demonstrate how he or she obtained a particular answer or performed a particular process, the teacher can identify the exact point of confusion and thus focus the corrective intervention very precisely. Teachers often re-teach an entire procedure when students have difficulties, starting from the beginning rather than dealing with the specific point of confusion and providing clarification and immediate practice on that point. When the whole procedure is re-taught some students still fail to recognise what they were doing wrong and so the difficulty continues (Westwood 1997).

Work samples can include written assignments in students' exercise books, projects, reports and portfolios. Portfolios have only recently become an accepted part of the assessment and recording system in mathematics, although they have a longer history in language arts, fine arts and design. The mathematics portfolio might contain such items as unique solutions to problems which the student has attempted, homework samples, drawings, diagrams, test sheets, teacher's checklists, newspaper and magazine cuttings and some interpretive writings. Samples of 'rough' workings may reveal the way in which strategies have been invented and tested when attempting difficult or unusual problems.

Van de Walle (1998) suggests that portfolios should also contain students' self-evaluation comments and reflections. According to Stenmark (1991), portfolios should focus on evidence of development in the student's thinking and the way in which the student has made connections between different topics and themes.

Error analysis

This diagnostic approach involves closely scrutinising students' written calculations in order to identify the types of errors that they have made. Obviously, a large collection of examples is needed before any firm conclusion can be made. Given an adequate sample of typical work, a pattern sometimes emerges, indicating a specific point of confusion that has led to the development of an incorrect response pattern when completing one step in an algorithm (Ashlock 1998). Sometimes, however, the errors appear to be fairly random, which may reflect either poor and inaccurate recall of basic number facts or a tendency to be distracted easily while working, thus losing track of the procedure.

Palmer et al. (1994) approach diagnosis and intervention from this error-analysis perspective. Their diagnostic program identifies 150 common errors made by students in number work and provides practical teaching advice on how to help students overcome the difficulty.

They broadly categorise students' errors as:

- problems with the number system:

  lining-up errors;

  regrouping errors;

  confusions with zeros;

  place-value difficulties;

- problems with algorithms:

  number facts;

  misunderstandings with operations or symbols;

  errors due to order of operations;

  problems with whole numbers and decimals;

- problems with fractions:

  difficulties with decimals;

  difficulties with vulgar fractions.

Serna and Patton (1997) use a less detailed analysis, and categorise errors only as:

- wrong operation (e.g. adding instead of multiplying);
- defective algorithm (one or more steps in the procedure are incorrect);
- basic number fact error within the calculation (e.g. 3 x 7 recalled as 28);
- place-value problem (often related to the defective algorithm category, but frequently including confusion over dealing with zeros at some point in an algorithm).

Although error analysis can be very valuable in identifying specific aspects of computation that require further attention, the aim of any intervention should be to help the student *understand* the process more effectively at a conceptual level, not merely to replace one trick with another at a rote-learned procedural level. Any conclusions based on evidence in students' work samples need to be followed up by an individual interview and discussion. It is necessary to listen to the student's own explanation of why he or she took a particular action at a specific point while solving a problem or working a calculation (Booker 1999).

Error analysis can be very time-consuming, and unless it leads to well-focused intervention there is a danger that it may become an end in itself. McCoy (1995, p. 374) reminds teachers that, 'the more simplified the data-collection process, the more likely it is that useful answers will be derived'. Even more important is the comment of Carter, Frobisher and Roper (1994, p. 124): 'Pupils do not set out to develop misconceptions and produce errors consciously ... difficulties and errors occur partly as a result of the performance of teachers'. Rather than approaching errors from the point of view of 'what's wrong with this student?' it is probably more productive for the teacher to consider 'how can I improve my instruction?'

Checklist of core knowledge and skills

It is recommended that teachers construct their own informal mathematics inventories containing a bank of test items that cover typical core concepts, knowledge and skills presented in previous school years, as well as essential subject matter from the current year. Such an inventory can be very useful in surveying quickly and effectively what any new student to the class already knows and what they need to be taught.

The following five levels of assessment, adapted from Westwood (1997), are designed to help a teacher obtain a fairly quick picture of a student's existing knowledge and skills in basic number. The first two levels are the most appropriate for assessing very young students or those with significant learning difficulties or disabilities. Later levels usually need to be supplemented by some curriculum-based tests in order to provide more detailed information concerning a student's procedural and conceptual knowledge. Note that the 'levels' are not related in any way to the levels of proficiency identified in the *Mathematics: a curriculum profile for Australian schools* (Australian Education Council 1994) (discussed below).

Level 1

At this level almost all the assessments will need to be done individually, working systematically through concrete and semi-concrete levels using appropriate materials such as toys, blocks, pictures, number cards, etc. Specific areas of knowledge and skill to be checked include whether the student can:

- rote-count 1 to 10 or 1 to 20;
- count sets of objects 1 to 5 or 1 to 10;
- produce equal sets of objects by one-to-one matching (up to 5 objects);
- recognise and name all numerals 1 to 10 or 11 to 20;
- demonstrate conservation of number on groups of up to 5 or 6 objects;
- place number symbols in correct sequence from 1 to 5 or 1 to 10;
- match correct numeral to number of objects in set: 1 to 5 or 1 to 10;
- write numerals 1 to 10;
- demonstrate an understanding of vocabulary such as 'count', 'more', 'how many', 'one more than', 'biggest', 'most', 'altogether', etc.

Level 2

Again, assessment at this level will require interview with the individual student. Concrete materials may also be needed for some of the following assessments if the student is unable to complete the tasks mentally. Can the student:

- perform simple addition with numbers below 10 using objects or fingers?
- answer simple oral questions on addition below 10?
- demonstrate recall of a few addition number facts below 10?
- use the 'count all' strategy for adding two sets?
- use the 'min' strategy (counting the smaller number on to the larger)?
- perform simple addition in written form (3 + 2 =)?
- demonstrate additive composition (e.g. 4 is 3 + 1, 2 + 2, 1 + 3, 4 + 0)?
- recognise and name all common coins and paper money?
- recite the days of the week?
- demonstrate understanding of simple ordinal value (e.g. 2nd, 4th)?
- perform simple subtraction with numbers below 10?
- correctly perform written subtraction of the type 8 – 3 = ?
- observe a simple operation with blocks and record it in written form?

Level 3

Some of the following tasks can be carried out with small groups of students. Simple paper-and-pencil, teacher-made tests or puzzles can be used to assess certain of the concepts or skills. Can the student:

- carry out simple mental addition and subtraction with numbers below 20?
- demonstrate a good recall of basic number facts (+ and –)?
- demonstrate the reversible character of addition and subtraction (e.g. 7 + 3 = 10, 10 – 7 = 3, 10 – 3 = 7)?

- perform both vertical and horizontal forms of simple addition below 20?
- perform vertical and horizontal forms of simple subtraction below 20?
- explain and demonstrate the commutative principle (order of items in addition does not matter)?
- use blocks or counters to translate a written number sentence into a concrete representation (e.g. 17 + 5 = 22; 25 − 20 = 5)?
- recognise numbers to 50? to 100?
- read the time on a digital clock?
- read the price correctly on an article in a shop?
- add simple amounts of money to $10? Mentally? In writing?
- recite the months of the year?

Level 4

Much of the assessment at this stage can be completed through group-administered paper-and-pencil tasks. Can the student:

- show good recall of + and − facts and some recall of basic x and ÷ facts?
- read and write numbers to 100? to 1000?
- give change to $20 by the counting-on method?
- recite the multiplication tables for x 2, x 5, x 10?
- recognise simple fractions such as $\frac{1}{2}$, $\frac{1}{4}$, 0.5?
- perform the written procedure for adding tens and units to tens and units (without regrouping and renaming, and with regrouping and renaming)?

Level 5

In assessing the computational skills below, the problems will look first at items requiring no regrouping, exchanging, etc. If the student is proficient at this level they should be tested on more difficult examples requiring regrouping. Can the student:

- demonstrate understanding of place value (e.g. the value of '6' in 6459)?
- perform the correct procedure for addition of HTU to HTU?
- perform the correct procedure for addition of HTU to ThHTU?
- perform the correct algorithm for multiplication (TU x TU, HTU x TU)?
- perform the correct algorithm for division (TU ÷ U; TU ÷ TU; HTU ÷ TU)?
- recall almost all basic number facts (+ − x ÷) with automaticity?

Beyond this point it is necessary to use more detailed assessment tools such as the *Mathematics: a curriculum profile for Australian schools*, or other appropriate testing resources listed in chapter 7.

The use of 'benchmarks' in numeracy assessment

'Benchmarks' are concise descriptions that indicate in a very general way what might be expected of students at a particular age level (Peach 1998). For example, the benchmarks in number for Years 3, 5 and 7 in Australian schools include the following knowledge, skills and strategies (abbreviated from Curriculum Corporation 1999). These are adapted examples only, and teachers need to consult the relevant benchmark documents for a much more comprehensive list, including sample assessment items.

Year 3

In situations and contexts relevant to the students' everyday lives they will be able to:

- read and record whole numbers up to three digits, and compare and order whole numbers up to two digits (e.g. enter a number on a calculator; say which of two numbers is larger; use numbers involving 100s meaningfully in their writing);

- use place-value knowledge to demonstrate different representations of the same two-digit number (e.g. say that 75 is the same as 7 tens and 5 ones; express numbers in different forms, such as 86 can be thought of as 8 tens and 6 ones, or 7 tens and 16 ones);

- show one-half involving collections and parts of a whole (e.g. show me half of 20 pencils; colour half of this strip of card);

- count up to 100 (forwards and backwards by 1s from any given number; forwards in 10s; forwards in multiples of 2s and 5s);

- identify patterns in numbers up to 100 (e.g. show that when counting in 5s or 10s the numbers end in 5 or 0);

- know, or work out mentally, basic addition facts to 10 + 10 and the related subtraction facts;

- use place value to mentally increase or decrease two-digit numbers by multiples of 10;

- add and subtract whole numbers in relevant problem-solving (mentally, in writing, or by using calculator, as appropriate) and check that answers are reasonable in the context;

- write calculations involving two-digit numbers with no regrouping (with a calculator, up to three digits provided the student can interpret the display);

- represent and solve simple multiplication problems involving equal groups or arrays (e.g. draw 2 rows of 5 chairs) and simple division problems involving sharing of repeated groups (e.g. share 12 counters evenly into 3 boxes);

- choose the relevant operation and apply appropriate strategies and computational skills in contexts relevant to students' everyday lives. Solving practical or real-life problems (e.g. 'We need 37 students to fill the seats on a bus. If we have 24 seats filled so far, how many more students are needed?'). Solve a one-step story and picture problem (e.g. 'There are 26 birds feeding on grass seeds. 12 flew away, so how many birds are left?');
- recognise coins and their values;
- use coins to represent amounts of money to $5;
- work out the value of a given set of coins to $5;
- compare the value of coins with the price of an item.

Year 5

In situations and contexts relevant to the students' everyday lives they will be able to:

- read, record, compare and order whole numbers up to four digits including Th, H, T and U (e.g. on a calculator; to record dates on a timeline);
- use place-value knowledge to demonstrate different representations of three- and four-digit numbers (e.g. that 740 has the same value as 74 x 10; express 408 as 39 tens and 18 ones; express 36 hundreds, 2 tens and 5 ones as three thousand six hundred and twenty-five);
- find a simple fraction of an object or a collection of objects (e.g. identify one-third of the cans in a carton, one-quarter of a length of rope, three-quarters of a pizza);
- read, record, compare and order decimal numbers to one or two decimal places (e.g. order pieces of rope that are 5.1 m, 1.5 m and 5 m in length; interpret decimal numbers on a calculator; explain that a bottle holding 1.25 L holds less than a 2 L bottle but more than a 1 L bottle);
- count forwards and backwards by 2s, 5s and 10s from any number to 100, and by 1s, 10s and 100s from any number to 1000;
- identify number patterns and sequences of numbers (e.g. What comes next? $46 - 9 = 37$, $56 - 9 = 47$, …);
- use a calculator to generate and continue such patterns as 0.2, 0.4, 0.6, 0.8 … or 100, 93, 86, …;
- use inverse relationship between addition and subtraction to check result from subtraction problems;
- know that the commutative principle does not apply to subtraction ($14 - 6$ is not the same as $6 - 14$);
- add and subtract whole numbers in relevant situations, using strategies appropriate to the task (mental, written, calculator); written methods with numbers up to three digits where regrouping is required; up to four digits with understanding of the display;

- estimate answers to addition and subtraction problems and judge reasonableness of results (e.g. judging that 493 is not reasonable when adding 117 and 76, that items costing $6.80 and $2.30 in the supermarket can be paid for with a $10 note);
- know, or work out mentally, basic multiplication facts to 10 x 10;
- multiply whole numbers (e.g. by making some use of basic facts: 6 x 3 = 18, so 6 x 30 = 180);
- carry out written multiplications, two-digit by one-digit numbers;
- use a calculator to investigate multiplication patterns or for computations which are beyond the student's mental and written limits;
- solve one-step problems involving whole numbers and money;
- add and subtract amounts of money (mentally for easy amounts, written methods for up to three-digit amounts with regrouping required, using a calculator for larger amounts).

Year 7

In situations and contexts relevant to the students' everyday lives they will be able to:

- read, record, compare and order numbers (using a calculator for large numbers, e.g. compare population figures for two cities; compare numbers with two decimal places; order numbers with decimals to two places);
- use place-value knowledge to demonstrate different representations of whole numbers and decimals to two places (e.g. know that 1.5 million is the same as 1 500 000; that 15 cents can be written as $0.15; that a height of 154 cm is the same as 1.54 m);
- read, record and compare simple common fractions (e.g. compare a simple fraction to a half, $\frac{3}{8}$ is less than half a pizza, $\frac{1}{3}$ is a larger share than $\frac{1}{4}$);
- recognise and use simple equivalent fractions, including decimals and percentage ($\frac{1}{2}$ = 50% = 0.5, $\frac{1}{4}$ = 25% = 0.25, '25% off' means the price is reduced by a quarter);
- interpret and use negative whole numbers (e.g. related to temperature as in –5°C; noting and recording a negative number on the calculator display);
- continue, analyse and create number patterns involving whole numbers, common fractions and decimals (e.g. skip counting 7, 14, 21, 28, …; count forwards or backwards 1.1, 1.0, 0.9, 0.8 …; count up $\frac{1}{3}$, $\frac{2}{3}$, 1, $1\frac{1}{3}$, ….; use place-value knowledge to continue sequence such as 2843, 2943, 3043, …);
- use a rule to create a set of numbers (e.g. the rule 'double and add 3' to complete the pattern (1 x 2) + 3 = 5, (5 x 2) + 3 = 13, (13 x 2) + 3 = 29, …);

- use the inverse relationship between addition and subtraction, and multiplication and division (e.g. to check calculations; to solve missing number problems; to simplify a calculation);

- recognise the various ways division can be expressed (e.g. $13 \div 4$, $13\frac{1}{4}$, $4\overline{)13}$;

- operate on whole numbers and decimals using the most appropriate approach (mental, written, calculator);

- estimate answers to computations;

- use common percentages (100%, 50%, 20%, 10%) in mental calculations;

- use proportional reasoning to solve problems involving ratio with whole numbers (e.g. a recipe for 4 people takes 1 cup of flour so for 8 people it will take …; if two drinks cost $5 how much for 10 drinks?);

- use number sense, appropriate strategies, computational skills and key information to solve problems (e.g. work out which is the best buy based on prices in an advertisement for different six-packs of soft drink cans).

Using the mathematics curriculum profiles

Outcomes and performance indicators in the *Mathematics: a curriculum profile for Australian schools* (Australian Education Council 1994) are different from the benchmarks in two main respects:

- they are not directly linked to age levels but refer to the types of performance students of any age level might display when they have reached or are reaching a particular stage of development;

- the indicators for any specific learning outcome are usually more detailed than benchmark statements and can therefore be of more practical value to the teacher when observing students engaged in mathematics lessons or when interviewing the student or assessing work samples and portfolios.

The *Mathematics: a curriculum profile for Australian schools* are organised into eight levels in ascending order of depth and complexity in terms of knowledge and proficiency. The sequence is regarded as a logical continuum of growth in mathematics learning, not specifically related to school-year levels or students' ages. The number strand for each developmental level is subdivided into the following skills and applications:

- counting and ordering;
- number patterns;
- equations;
- applying numbers;
- mental computation;
- written computation;
- calculator uses.

Some examples taken from the number strand of the *Mathematics: a curriculum profile for Australian schools* are presented below. Teachers are referred to the profile document for the outcomes and indicators for other main mathematics curricular areas such as space, measurement, chance and data, and algebra. The examples here are adapted and abbreviated from Level 1 and Level 5 in 'Number', merely to provide some indication of the increase in complexity between the two levels. Indications of proficiency are described fully in the profile document, with examples.

Level 1

At this level a student can:

- count and estimate collections, order two or more collections, and order things within collections;
- copy, continue and invent repeating and counting patterns and use numbers to represent those patterns;
- represent self-generated or orally presented number stories involving small numbers using materials or drawings;
- understand that money is used in exchange for goods;
- use counting and other means of mentally solving self-generated or orally presented questions from stories involving small numbers;
- use a calculator to represent and explore simple number relationships.

Level 5

By Level 5 the student can:

- interpret and use whole powers, square roots and straightforward ratios and percentages;
- choose and sequence several operations covering situations with decimal multipliers and divisors and division of smaller by larger numbers;
- estimate and calculate mentally with whole numbers, money and simple fractions, including multiplying and dividing some two-digit numbers by one-digit numbers;
- use and understand written methods to add, subtract, multiply and divide whole numbers and common and decimal fractions (whole-number multipliers and divisors);
- make efficient use of a calculator for common and decimal fractions and percentages and take into account orders of operations.

Teacher-made tests

In many subject areas the regular setting of tests has become unpopular. Current ideology suggests that students' abilities should be assessed mainly by observation and from samples of typical work. Effective teachers do, however, make use of tests for diagnostic purposes and to measure achievement of objectives. Research previously cited in this book indicates that regular use of testing results in higher attainment in mathematics than occurs in classes where there is no use of testing. The research also suggests, on the other hand, that too much testing can be counterproductive.

Teacher-made tests should be directly linked to the precise performance objectives (behavioural objectives) set for that unit of work. The objectives should indicate not only what the student must be able to demonstrate, but also to what standard or criterion (e.g. at least 8 out of 10, 100% correct, etc.) and under what conditions (e.g. no time restriction, without the use of a calculator).

When teachers design tests to cover the work taught in their classes (curriculum-based tests), the ideal test should have the following features:

- the test begins with a few easy items to allow even the least-able students to experience some feeling of success;
- at least two, and preferably three, items are provided at the same level of difficulty to enable careless errors to be differentiated from those that are persistent;
- a variety of question formats to make the test more interesting (e.g. some multiple-choice, some 'missing numbers', some calculations in which the workings must be shown, some drawing or measuring);
- the content tested should relate to the actual topics covered;
- unless the test is designed to assess only computational skills, it should contain interesting problems that will allow the students' levels of reasoning to be evaluated, and provide evidence of the students' conceptual and strategic knowledge.

Diagnostic tests

It should be clear that almost all the assessment procedures described above can yield useful diagnostic information in addition to answering the basic question, 'Can the student do this task successfully?' Assessment should help to uncover the reasons why a student is having difficulties with a particular concept, process or strategy.

The four key questions to use as a framework for assessing individual students are:

1. What can the student already do without assistance?

This reflects the student's current knowledge, skills and strategies.

2. What can the student do if given some degree of support or guidance?

This is a clear indication of which concepts and skills can soon be taught as priorities within that student's zone of proximal development.

3. What gaps exist in the student's previous learning?

Often specific gaps can be detected, due perhaps to absences from school, changing schools, having a less than effective teacher during one year, etc.

4. What does the student need to be taught next as a top priority in their program?

Identify the most important knowledge, skills or strategies to be taught next, building on the foundations of the student's current abilities.

Answers to these four questions may be obtained from most of the approaches described in this chapter, including direct observation, examining work samples, formal or informal testing, and individual discussions with the student.

There are three levels of abstraction involved in diagnostic assessment. Identification of the level at which the student is operating will help the teacher to answer the question, 'What can the student do when given some degree of support and guidance?' The three levels are:

- concrete — can the student solve the problem if permitted to use real objects, or to act it out?

- semi-concrete/semi-abstract — can the student perform the process with blocks, tally marks, fingers, etc.?

- abstract — can the student complete the process using symbols alone, or carry out the computation mentally?

During the diagnostic assessment of a student the teacher may need to move up or down this hierarchy from concrete to abstract in an attempt to determine the level at which the student is operating in different areas of mathematics. Assessment should also reveal the extent to which the student approaches mathematics at a purely procedural level, or whether he or she is developing a sound conceptual understanding (McCoy 1995).

Closely related to the error-analysis procedures described earlier are the many diagnostic number tests that have been developed. Most of these tests are based on task analysis of the steps involved in completing computational algorithms at different levels of difficulty. For example, a division test would begin with a small single-digit divisor and a dividend no greater than 10, then progress in carefully graded steps until large numbers are being divided by large numbers. The aim of using such tests is to identify the point at which a student begins to have difficulty, so that teaching can commence at that point.

A very useful example of this type of assessment tool is Doig's (1991) *Diagnostic mathematics profiles*. These four test-sheets can be used to assess an individual student, or can be applied to a whole class for screening purposes. The processes of addition, subtraction, multiplication and division are covered. One very valuable feature of the test is that each level of proficiency is linked with a specific performance objective, so the teacher can use the results to identify which objectives need to be included next in a student's program.

Appendix 2 shows the One Minute Basic Number Facts Tests, with Australian norms. These tests are useful for quick screening of whole classes. The results also allow rapid identification of students whose slowness and difficulties in most areas of basic mathematics and problem-solving may be due to lack of automaticity in their recall of the most basic number facts. These simple tests can also be used in diagnostic assessment of individual students.

7 Recommended resources

Texts

Beesey, C. & Davie, L. (1994). *Math talk: understanding and using the language of mathematics*. Melbourne: Macmillan.

The title says it all. The important role of language in learning and communicating about mathematics is made explicit. The book provides a very practical resource for teachers, including photocopiable blackline masters. The curriculum coverage extends beyond what we normally regard as 'numeracy', but there is plenty to talk and write about in the various sections.

Bley, N.S. & Thornton, C.A. (1995). *Teaching mathematics to students with learning disablities* (3rd edn). Austin: ProEd.

This is an excellent resource for regular class teachers, support teachers and tutors. While having sufficient theory and research underpinning it, the text is almost entirely devoted to practical suggestions for making mathematics easier to learn for the hard-to-teach student. Unlike many books on teaching mathematics to students with learning difficulties, this text devotes a great deal of attention to the important topic of problem-solving.

Booker, G., Bond, D., Briggs, J. & Davey, G. (1997). *Teaching primary mathematics* (2nd edn). Melbourne: Addison Wesley Longman.

If teachers only ever purchase one text dealing with learning and teaching basic mathematics, this would have to rank highly among their best options. In over 400 pages the authors present a very comprehensive coverage of contemporary views on children's learning, effective teaching approaches, curriculum content, assessment and recording. The text is well-illustrated with graphics depicting specific teaching strategies, aids and algorithms. In particular, the helpful ways in which Dienes' MAB materials and 'bundles of ten' are used to develop an understanding of place value, regrouping, renaming and exchanging are well-illustrated.

Brown, T. (1998). *Coordinating mathematics across the primary school*. London: Falmer.

This book is a valuable guide for any teacher with some school-wide responsibility for ensuring that mathematics teaching is effective. The author deals with issues of how children learn mathematics and how teaching methods and style of instruction influence learning. Recent changes in approach are discussed, with particular reference to the ways in which the curriculum is developed and delivered. Important issues are explored, such as professional development needs of staff, policy-making, management of resources, curriculum planning, assessment and parental involvement. The text presents a good, balanced approach to pedagogy. Readers will find much that agrees with the perspective taken in *Numeracy and Learning Difficulties.*

Burns, M. (1998). *About teaching mathematics: a K–8 resource*. Sausalito, Calif.: Maths Solutions Publications.

Marilyn Burns is perhaps one of the most published authors of practical, down-to-earth advice for mathematics teachers. Her articles frequently appear in professional teacher education journals. In this text Burns takes problem-solving as the starting point and shows how the specific skills of arithmetic can be acquired and practised through such an approach. Teachers will find this book useful and easy to read. They will also find useful the brief article by Burns, 'Can I balance arithmetic instruction with real-life math?' This is an excellent source of sound advice on the essential role of basic number facts, mental computation and the use of the calculator, in contemporary 'real-life math' programs. See *The Instructor*, 107(7) 1998: 55–8.

Chinn, S.J. & Ashcroft, J.R. (1998). *Mathematics for dyslexics: a teaching handbook* (2nd edn). London: Whurr.

The authors have collated a set of practical ideas for assisting students with major learning difficulties to cope more effectively with mathematics. A valuable feature of the book is that almost every strategy described is also well-illustrated, thus providing both student and teacher (or tutor) with a visual representation of the procedure, concept or model.

Donlan, C. (ed.) (1998). *The development of mathematical skills*. Hove: Erlbaum.

This book provides an excellent overview of current knowledge and theory about the acquisition of numeracy and basic mathematical skills. In addition to a survey of the early development of number skills and concepts in children, the various contributors also discuss specific difficulties and factors that can impair normal mathematical growth. Issues of anxiety and its impact on working memory are explored, as are the problems of learning in students who are deaf, language-impaired or specifically learning-disabled. While certainly not a beginner's text, this book is an invaluable resource for anyone commencing research in this area.

Heddens, J.W. & Speer, W. R. (1995). *Today's mathematics concepts and classroom methods* (8th edn). Columbus: Prentice Hall.

This two-volume set covers all basic concepts of teaching and learning mathematics, classroom methods and instructional activities. Along with the books by Booker et al. (1997) and Reys et al. (1998) listed here, this text is also extremely comprehensive, research-based and of real practical value to both beginning teachers and those with experience. Highly recommended.

Mulligan, J. & Mitchelmore, M. (eds) (1996). *Children's number learning*. Adelaide: Australian Association of Mathematics Teachers.

This book contains contributions from many leading mathematics educators in Australia. It provides an excellent starting point for any teacher or student teacher wishing to explore in more detail what is currently known about children's acquisition of number sense and their development of procedural and conceptual knowledge. Main sections examine the development of counting skills, place value, computational strategies and knowledge of fractions. Of particular interest are the chapters on the use of problem-solving in the early years, and children's various strategies for solving different types of problems.

Pound, L. (1999). *Supporting mathematical development in the early years*. Buckingham: Open University Press.

A very clearly written and reader-friendly introduction to the ways in which young children begin to build number concepts and skills, largely from incidental learning and exploration. The writer discusses how a child's natural interests in quantitative learning experiences can be optimised by subtle adult and peer interactions. The curricular issues and teaching approaches are well-supported by reference to relevant research.

Reys, R., Suydam, M., Lindquist, M. & Smith, N. (1998). *Helping children learn mathematics* (5th edn). Boston: Allyn & Bacon.

Any book that can reach a fifth edition has obviously proved its worth. Teachers have found this text to be comprehensive, balanced and practical. Although the writers are American, the concepts and strategies presented are equally applicable in the Australian context. This book is used as the basic text for teacher education courses in a number of Australian universities.

Riedesel, C.A. & Schwartz, J.E. (1999). *Essentials of elementary mathematics* (2nd edn). Boston: Allyn & Bacon.

A well-written and wide-ranging book which not only visits the key areas of knowledge embraced by the term 'numeracy' but also explores the factors that influence mathematics curricula. The authors advocate balance in teaching approaches, and highlight the importance of considering the characteristics of students, as well as curriculum matter, when planning and implementing high-quality programs. They provide teachers with useful teaching strategies.

Wahl, M. (1997). *Math for humans: teaching math through the seven intelligences*. Langley, Wash.: LivnLern Press.

If teachers believe in the value of the seven intelligences model, this text will appeal to them. It covers such issues as learning styles in mathematics, dealing with anxiety, sharpening math facts, mastering the basic operations and cooperative learning.

Assessment and teaching resources

Booker, G. (1994). *Booker profiles in mathematics*. Melbourne: Australian Council for Educational Research.

This diagnostic test uses visual material in easel-presentation format to enable a teacher or psychologist to assess the numeration and computational skills of an individual. The content is appropriate for students ranging in age from early primary school to adult. The main purpose of the assessment is to discover, in the case of individuals with learning difficulties, precisely what they can and cannot do, in order to plan an appropriate intervention program.

Brown, G. (1992). *Related maths facts*. Sydney: Macquarie University Special Education Centre.

This program teaches the concepts of addition and subtraction simultaneously, and introduces all addition and subtraction facts for a particular number. Through demonstration with physical objects first, students are led to understand and practise essential basic facts to the point of mastery. It is an excellent resource for students with learning difficulties, but only as an adjunct to the broader content of the mathematics curriculum.

Brown, V., Cronin, J. & McEntire, E. (1994). *Test of mathematical abilities (revised) (TOMA–2)*. Austin: ProEd.

Designed for use with US grades 3 to 12, the five subtests explore students' vocabulary, computational skills, general information and word problem-solving. Assessment can also be made of a student's attitude toward mathematics as a subject. All sections other than 'general information' can, if necessary, be administered to groups of students. Results can be interpreted cautiously from standard scores, percentiles, age equivalents and grade equivalents, but these are based only on US populations.

Bryant, D. & Driscoll, M. (1998). *Exploring classroom assessment in mathematics*. Alexandria: Association for Supervision and Curriculum Development.

The focus in this short US text is how teachers can become skilled in the more dynamic types of assessment necessary to evaluate children's problem-solving and investigative strategies. It is based on a teacher-workshop model and can be used as a valuable in-service teacher education guide. The types of assessment described relate most closely to group observations, interviews and work samples, as discussed in this book. The text also provides an annotated bibliography of related resources.

Connolly, A. (1998). *Key math* (rev. edn). Circle Pines, Minn.: American Guidance Service.

This US assessment kit is fairly well-known in Australia, particularly by educational psychologists who may use it when carrying out a detailed psycho-educational evaluation of a student referred for learning or behaviour difficulties. It is an individually administered test, using easel-picture format for presentation of each item. Fourteen subtests are used to assess proficiency across three broad categories of content, operations and applications. The subtests explore numeration, fractions, geometry, addition, subtraction, multiplication, mental computation, numerical reasoning, word problems, missing elements, money, measurement and time. Appendix A of the 1998 edition contains a very useful set of behavioural objectives covering each of the areas of knowledge and skill tapped by the subtests. This information can lead smoothly to program planning. Age range is regarded as US K to grade 8. It must be noted that administration of key math can be quite time-consuming and, unless very good use will be made of the results, teachers often find that their own curriculum-based tests yield more immediately useful data.

Doig, B. (1995). *Activities and assessment in mathematics (AAIM)*. Melbourne: Australian Council for Educational Research.

This is a learning and informal assessment instrument suitable for the upper primary and lower secondary age range. The activities provided in AAIM link directly with Levels 3 and 4 in the *Mathematics: a curriculum profile for Australian schools*, and cover all five key strands. Over 200 photocopiable classroom activities can be used by teachers to observe and evaluate students' conceptual and procedural knowledge.

Enzensberger, H.M. (1998). *The number devil: a mathematical adventure*. New York: Metropolitan Books.

Why not take maths well and truly into a language arts lesson? This delightful story will do that. I guarantee that even the most 'anti-maths' language arts teacher will love this one. The publishers say, 'Author Hans Magnus Enzensberger's dry humour and sense of wonder will keep you and your kids entranced while you learn (shhh!) mathematical principles'. Age ten years to adult. I loved it!

Freeman, L. & Outhred, L. (1994). *Building basic facts skills package*. Sydney: Macquarie University Special Education Centre.

A supplementary resource to help students with difficulties in the four basic number operations. Student worksheets provide paper-and-pencil activities to link pictorial and symbolic representation.

Freeman, L. & Outhred, L. (1994). *Computational skills package*. Sydney: Macquarie University Special Education Centre.

This package is intended to be used as a supplementary resource to help children who are having difficulty with more complex computational skills. The program includes individual placement tests for each of the four processes, and daily recording charts.

Ginsburg, H.P., Jacobs, S.F. & Lopez, L. (1998*). The teacher's guide to flexible interviewing in the classroom*. Boston: Allyn & Bacon.

This book helps teachers gain skills in using teaching situations, together with group and individual interviewing, to uncover children's quality of thinking when engaging in mathematical tasks. In particular, it helps teachers to improve their questioning skills so that an assessment situation becomes a learning situation for teachers as well as for students.

Kirkby, D. (1995). *Numbers*. Oxford: Heinemann.

A colourful, well-illustrated students' resource book, but much in it is valuable to teachers too. Part of the Maths Alive series, it covers basic number concepts and the four key operations. Attention is also given in a very visual way to factors, prime numbers, squared numbers, fractions, rounding up, rounding down, and positive and negative numbers (and yes, answers are provided!).

Mason, K., Hagues, N. & Patilla, P. (1998). *Mathematics twelve* (2nd edn). Windsor: NFER-Nelson.

This is the first level of three tests in the series Mathematics 12–14. It was designed in Britain and contains fifty questions that can be group-administered to students aged eleven to thirteen. There are two main sections in the students' booklet. In the first section, but not in the second, students may use a calculator. The test samples knowledge and skills in number, measurement, algebra, space and shape, handling data and probability. In the number section the following aspects are assessed: number patterns, place value, properties of numbers, rounding, money problems, fractions, decimals and ratio or proportion. The answer booklets are clearly set out and user-friendly. Norms are provided, but they relate to students in Britain.

Palmer, D., Kays, M., Smith, A. & Doig, B. (1994). *Stop! look and lesson*. Melbourne: Australian Council for Educational Research.

This book was referred to in chapter 6. The authors of this diagnostic program suggest that students' errors are seldom haphazard; they reflect quite clearly the misconceptions students have developed. If teachers identify the types of error accurately, their chances of helping students overcome the difficulties through well-directed teaching are greatly enhanced. One volume in the set comprises the manual to guide the error diagnosis. The second volume clearly illustrates more than sixty strategies for dealing with the problem and building success and confidence through practice.

Recht, E., Forster, M. & Masters, G. (1998). *Developmental assessment resource for teachers: DART mathematics*. Melbourne: Australian Council for Educational Research.

This interesting and stimulating assessment kit is suitable for upper primary and lower secondary students in Australia. It covers concepts and skills usually identified in Levels 2 to 5 in the *Mathematics: a curriculum profile for Australian schools*. Many of the interpretations that can be made from the results of individual students can be mapped directly onto the profiles for reporting purposes. The main curriculum strands covered by DART are number and number sense, space and spatial sense, measurement, chance and data, and data sense. The assessment process is carried out using a realistic context depicted on videotape ('Maths at the zoo'). Answer booklets for each strand can be photocopied. Calculators can be used for only the first part of the test. Results can be presented descriptively in terms of knowledge and skills the student clearly possesses, and their actual performance can be charted on a profile sheet.

Schleiger, H.E. & Gough, J. (1993). *Diagnostic mathematical tasks: prep to grade 6*. Geelong: Deakin University Press.

The main feature of this set of assessment tests for the early and middle primary years is that almost all the problems are presented in pictorial format. Oral questioning is used in the early years, thus making it possible to assess students' numeracy skills and concepts relatively separately from their reading ability. Another helpful resource is the diagnostic chart for each year level that allows teachers to identify specific areas of weakness across different types of question.

Useful journals

Equals: mathematics and special educational needs
> Four issues a year
> Contact: Mathematical Association
> 259 London Road
> Leicester LE2 3BE, UK

Focus on learning problems in mathematics
> Four issues a year
> Contact: Centre for Teaching and Learning Mathematics
> PO Box 3149
> Framingham, Mass. 01701, USA

Mathematics in school
> Five issues a year
> Contact: NCTM
> 1906 Association Drive
> Reston, VA 20191 – 1593, USA

Teaching children mathematics
> Nine issues a year
> Contact: NCTM
> 1906 Association Drive
> Reston, VA 20191 – 1593, USA

Appendices

The city of Trantville
exactly 200 km north
Butan is 90 km due e
Approximately how far
from Seatown?

Appendix 1

Students with learning difficulties: selecting priority curriculum content

While the main focus of this book has been on reducing learning failure by providing high-quality instruction *within the mainstream classroom*, it acknowledges that some students with learning difficulties may need a modified mathematics program. Some may also receive additional tuition in mathematics, either through a support service within the school or through after-hours private tutoring. A few students may have significant disabilities and attend special schools or receive modified programs within mainstream classrooms. For such students the content of the mathematics curriculum must address the functional uses to which number skills are put in everyday life, but it should also attend to the creative and recreational aspects of number, no matter how simple and basic. The program for students with intellectual disability, for example, must be enriching and enjoyable as well as purely functional, and it must be taught effectively to ensure success (Johnson 1999).

This appendix provides a brief list of some of the curriculum content considered to comprise the essential core of functional numeracy. Trying to decide upon core content for a mathematics curriculum for students with learning difficulties is helped by the results of surveys of community expectations of basic numeracy (e.g. Knight et al. 1995; Patton et al. 1997). Parents and employers agree that the key areas for functional numeracy are:

- counting;
- multiplication tables;
- use of the four basic processes (particularly + and –);
- money management;
- time;
- measurement;
- some grasp of everyday common fractions and decimal fractions;
- the ability to understand simple charts, graphs and tables.

Based on the identified priorities, the list below suggests a core of curriculum content basic to the everyday needs of non-academic school-leavers. Items marked with an asterisk are desirable, but could be omitted for students with severe learning difficulties and intellectual disabilities.

There is always a danger that when a core list is presented in any subject area teachers may tend to regard it as 'the curriculum', and limit their instruction to the skills and concepts listed. This is not the intention here, and teachers should refer to documents such as those describing the benchmarks for specific age levels, and to the *National statement on mathematics for Australian schools*, in order to identify additional content that will extend every child as far as possible.

Number skills

- rote-counting ability;
- ability to count groups of objects accurately;
- reading and writing of numbers;
- understanding of cardinal and ordinal aspects of number;
- a high degree of automaticity in recall of basic number facts;
- ability to carry out the four basic processes in arithmetic, with emphasis on addition and subtraction;
- appreciation of place value;
- counting in intervals (2s, 5s, 10s, 20s, 50s, 100s);
- grouping objects (e.g. How many groups of 4 in 22? How many left over?);
- ability to use a calculator or table-chart for multiplication and division;
- ability to estimate reasonable results for real-life calculations;
- basic problem-solving strategies, using the four processes.

Money

- coin and note recognition;
- ability to manage money (e.g. count up total amounts using coins and notes; give change by 'counting-on' method; use different combinations of coins and notes to achieve a given total);
- ability to perform basic processes with dollars and cents (especially + and –);
- experiences with simple budgeting and banking;
- basic problem-solving involving money (with and without calculator).

Fractions, decimals and percentages

- understanding and recognition of simple common fractions ($\frac{1}{2}$, $\frac{3}{4}$, $\frac{1}{4}$, $\frac{1}{10}$);
- simple + and – operations with like fractions;*
- equivalence of some simple fractions (e.g. $\frac{1}{2} = \frac{5}{10} = 0.5$);*
- decimal notation: tenths (and hundredths*) particularly in connection with measurement (linear, temperature, etc.) and money;
- awareness of meaning of 100%, 50%, 25%, 10%;
- problem-solving and applications involving + and – with simple fractions, decimals and percentages in everyday contexts.

Measurement and data

- ability to measure and construct using mm, cm and m;
- awareness of distance (km);*
- ability to weigh in g and kg;*
- awareness of common weights of goods (e.g. packet of sugar, potatoes);
- ability to tell the time (both digital and analogue);
- applications of concepts of time (e.g. estimating how long it will take to do a certain task, or to travel a certain journey, or to get to the bus stop);
- knowing days of the week, months of the year, and seasons;
- liquid measures (L), e.g. related to petrol, cans of paint, carton of milk or juice, etc.;*
- temperature (ability to read thermometer);*
- use of measurement and scale in such topics as simple map work and diagrams;*
- ability to interpret simple graphs and charts;*
- application of all the above knowledge, skills, concepts and processes to solving a variety of problems across the curriculum.

Note: * = items that might be omitted for students with severe learning difficulties.

Appendix 2

The One Minute Basic Number Facts Tests (1995)

The *One Minute Basic Number Facts Tests* are based on the performance of students in South Australian government schools in 1995. All scores in the norm tables have been rounded to the nearest 0.5 or nearest whole number.

In the norm tables the 'normal range' column indicates the range of scores within which roughly 50% of the students in that particular age group would score. This range has been determined by using ±.68 standard deviation.

The 'critically low score' has been calculated from one standard deviation below the mean for the age group. Scores below this critical level place a student in approximately the bottom 16% of students in that age group.

The test-retest reliability of the One Minute Basic Number Facts Tests ranges from .88 to .94 according to age level.

Instructions for administration

- Ensure that the test material has been prepared using a size of type large enough for the children to read easily. If necessary, enlarge the test on a photocopier and, for young children or those with coordination difficulties, considerably increase the space between test items.

- Administer at most only two tests at a time, with a break (e.g. recess) between the addition/subtraction tests and the multiplication/division tests. The multiplication and division tests would not normally be given to children below the age of seven years.

- Place the test sheet face down on the children's tables.

- The children write their name on the back of the sheet.

- You will later need to check the children's age in years and months.

- Say:
  'When you turn over the page you will find some addition (etc.) questions.

  When I say "start now" I want you to write down the answer to each question as quickly as you can. Don't worry if you don't finish them all.

  Work down the page.

  Pencils ready. Now turn over the page.

  Find the addition (adding) questions.'

  As soon as the children are ready, say 'Start now'.

- After exactly one minute say '**Stop!** Pencils down'.

- Repeat the procedure for the subtraction test.

- Say 'Don't forget, this is subtraction. You are taking the number away this time. One minute, starting now'.

- After one minute say '**Stop!** Pencils down'.

One Minute Tests of Basic Number Facts

Addition	Subtraction	Multiplication	Division
2 + 1 =	2 − 1 =	1 x 2 =	2 ÷ 1 =
1 + 4 =	5 − 1 =	2 x 3 =	4 ÷ 2 =
2 + 2 =	3 − 2 =	2 x 5 =	3 ÷ 1 =
4 + 2 =	5 − 3 =	1 x 4 =	6 ÷ 3 =
3 + 4 =	6 − 2 =	3 x 2 =	8 ÷ 2 =
2 + 3 =	2 − 2 =	4 x 3 =	9 ÷ 3 =
5 + 2 =	6 − 4 =	9 x 1 =	10 ÷ 2 =
4 + 5 =	7 − 2 =	6 x 2 =	12 ÷ 3 =
3 + 5 =	6 − 1 =	3 x 4 =	15 ÷ 5 =
2 + 8 =	7 − 3 =	5 x 3 =	16 ÷ 4 =
4 + 4 =	8 − 2 =	7 x 2 =	18 ÷ 3 =
2 + 5 =	7 − 5 =	3 x 6 =	20 ÷ 4 =
3 + 3 =	6 − 6 =	2 x 8 =	21 ÷ 3 =
1 + 8 =	8 − 3 =	4 x 5 =	24 ÷ 4 =
6 + 4 =	7 − 4 =	9 x 2 =	30 ÷ 3 =
3 + 7 =	9 − 3 =	3 x 7 =	30 ÷ 5 =
6 + 3 =	8 − 5 =	6 x 4 =	24 ÷ 8 =
5 + 5 =	9 − 5 =	3 x 9 =	27 ÷ 3 =
1 + 5 =	9 − 9 =	8 x 3 =	50 ÷ 5 =
6 + 2 =	10 − 4 =	7 x 0 =	28 ÷ 4 =
2 + 7 =	9 − 4 =	8 x 4 =	32 ÷ 8 =
4 + 6 =	10 − 3 =	5 x 6 =	35 ÷ 5 =
5 + 7 =	11 − 2 =	4 x 7 =	42 ÷ 6 =
8 + 3 =	10 − 6 =	8 x 6 =	45 ÷ 5 =
4 + 9 =	12 − 3 =	7 x 5 =	48 ÷ 8 =
7 + 6 =	12 − 6 =	9 x 4 =	54 ÷ 6 =
6 + 6 =	15 − 5 =	8 x 9 =	36 ÷ 9 =
8 + 6 =	11 − 5 =	7 x 7 =	56 ÷ 7 =
9 + 8 =	13 − 3 =	6 x 9 =	64 ÷ 8 =
6 + 9 =	12 − 9 =	8 x 8 =	63 ÷ 9 =
8 + 7 =	14 − 6 =	6 x 8 =	72 ÷ 8 =
9 + 5 =	17 − 8 =	9 x 9 =	81 ÷ 9 =
9 + 7 =	16 − 9 =	9 x 7 =	88 ÷ 8 =

Numeracy and Learning Difficulties: Approaches to teaching and assessment

Norm tables for the basic number facts tests

Addition

Age (years)	Average score	Normal range	Critically low score
6.0	4.0	2 – 6	0
6.5	5.5	3 – 7	2
7.0	8.0	5 – 11	3
7.5	11.0	7 – 15	5
8.0	12.0	8 – 16	6
8.5	15.5	11 – 19	9
9.0	17.0	13 – 21	10
9.5	18.5	14 – 22	11
10.0	20.5	16 – 24	13
10.5	21.5	16 – 26	14
11.0	23.5	20 – 27	18

Subtraction

Age (years)	Average score	Normal range	Critically low score
6.0	3.0	1 – 5	0
6.5	4.0	2 – 6	1
7.0	6.5	3 – 9	2
7.5	8.0	5 – 11	3
8.0	9.0	6 – 12	4
8.5	12.0	8 – 16	6
9.0	13.0	9 – 17	7
9.5	15.0	11 – 19	8
10.0	16.5	12 – 21	10
10.5	18.0	13 – 23	11
11.0	21.0	17 – 25	14

Multiplication

Age (years)	Average score	Normal range	Critically low score
7.5	4.0	1 – 7	0
8.0	5.5	3 – 8	2
8.5	8.5	5 – 11	3
9.0	9.0	6 – 12	4
9.5	11.5	7 – 15	5
10.0	13.0	9 – 17	7
10.5	15.0	10 – 20	8
11.0	17.0	13 – 21	11

Division

Age (years)	Average score	Normal range	Critically low score
7.5	2.5	0 – 4	0
8.0	3.0	1 – 5	0
8.5	5.0	2 – 8	1
9.0	6.0	3 – 9	1
9.5	7.0	3 – 11	2
10.0	9.0	5 – 13	3
10.5	11.0	6 – 16	3
11.0	13.0	8 – 18	5

References

Abele, A. (1998). Reasoning processes and the quality of reasoning. In F. Seeger, J. Voigt & U. Waschjescio (eds), *The culture of the mathematics classroom.* (pp. 127–57). Cambridge: Cambridge University Press.

Adhami, M. (1999). The challenge of whole-class teaching. *Equals: Mathematics and Special Educational Needs*, 5(2): 5–8.

Airasian, P. & Walsh, M. (1997). Constructivist cautions. *Phi Delta Kappan*, 78(6): 444–9.

Alexander, R.J. (1995). *Versions of primary education*. London: Routledge.

Anderson, R.C. (1984). Some reflections on the acquisition of knowledge. *Educational Researcher*, 13(9): 5–10.

Ashlock, R.B. (1998). *Error patterns in computation* (7th edn). Upper Saddle River, NJ: Merrill.

Aubrey, C. (1999). Maths for the millennium. *Special Children* (supplement), 122: 1–8.

Australian Education Council (1991). *A national statement on mathematics for Australian schools*. Melbourne: Curriculum Corporation.

Australian Education Council (1994). *Mathematics: a curriculum profile for Australian schools*. Melbourne: Curriculum Corporation.

Baroody, A.J. (1993). Fostering the mathematical learning of young children. In B. Spodek (ed.), *Handbook of research on the education of young children* (pp. 151–75). New York: Macmillan.

Baroody, A.J. & Standifer, D.J. (1993). Addition and subtraction in the primary grades. In R.J. Jensen (ed.), *Research ideas for the classroom: early childhood mathematics* (pp. 72–102). New York: Macmillan.

Battista, M.T. (1999). The mathematical miseducation of America's youth: ignoring research and scientific study in education. *Phi Delta Kappan*, 80(6): 425–33.

Bay, J., Beem, J., Reys, R., Papick, I. & Barnes, D. (1999). Student reactions to standards-based mathematics curricula: the interplay between curriculum, teachers and students. *School Science and Mathematics*, 99(4): 182–7.

Beaty, J.J. (1998). *Observing development of the young child* (4th edn). Upper Saddle River, NJ: Merrill.

Bell, G. (1995). A cross-cultural study of mathematical thinking. In G. Bell (ed.), *Review of mathematics education in Asia and the Pacific* (pp. 143–52). Lismore, NSW: Southern Cross Mathematical Association.

Benjamin, G.R. (1997). *Japanese lessons*. New York: University of New York Press.

Bishop, W. (1999). The California mathematics standards. *Phi Delta Kappan*, 80(6): 439–40.

Bjorklund, D.F. (1995). *Children's thinking: developmental function and individual differences* (2nd edn). Pacific Grove, CA: Brooks-Cole.

Bley, N.S. & Thornton, C.A. (1995). *Teaching mathematics to students with learning disabilities* (3rd edn). Austin: ProEd.

Boaler, J. (1997). *Experiencing school mathematics*. Buckingham: Open University Press.

Booker, G. (1994). *Booker profiles in mathematics*. Melbourne: Australian Council for Educational Research.

Booker, G. (1999). Numeracy in action: diagnosis and intervention in mathematics. In W. Scott & P. Westwood (eds), *Learning disabilities: advocacy and action* (pp. 39–51). Melbourne: AREA Press.

Booker, G., Bond, D., Briggs, J. & Davey, G. (1997). *Teaching primary mathematics* (2nd edn). Melbourne: Addison Wesley Longman.

Borasi, R. (1996). *Reconceiving mathematics instruction: a focus on errors*. Norwood, NJ: Ablex Publishing.

Boulton-Lewis, G. & Tait, K. (1994). Young children's representations and strategies for addition. *British Journal of Educational Psychology*, 64: 231–42.

Broomes, D. & Petty, O. (1995). Mathematical problem-solving, modelling and application. In D. Broomes, G. Cumberbatch, A. James & O. Petty (eds), *Teaching primary school mathematics* (pp. 73–102). Kingston: Ian Randle for UNESCO.

Brown, A.L. & Palincsar, A.S. (1989). Guided, cooperative learning and individual knowledge acquisition. In L.B. Resnick (ed.), *Knowing, learning, and instruction* (pp. 393–451). Hillsdale, NJ: Erlbaum.

Brown, T. (1998). *Coordinating mathematics across the primary school*. London: Falmer.

Bruner, J. (1960). *The process of education*. Cambridge: Harvard University Press.

Bruner, J. (1966). *Toward a theory of instruction*. Cambridge: Harvard University Press.

Bryant, D. & Driscoll, M. (1998). *Exploring classroom assessment in mathematics*. Alexandria: Association for Supervision and Curriculum Development.

Burns, M. (1993). The twelve most important things you can do to be a better math teacher. *The Instructor*, 102(8): 28–31.

Burton, L. (ed.) (1994a). *Who counts? Assessing mathematics in Europe*. Stoke-on-Trent: Trentham Books.

Burton, L. (1994b). *Children learning mathematics: patterns and relationships*. Hemel Hempstead: Simon & Schuster.

Butterworth, B. (1999). *What counts: how every brain is hardwired for math*. New York: Free Press.

Buxton, L. (1991). *Math panic*. Portsmouth, NH: Heinemann.

Carpenter, T.P., Fennema, E., Peterson, P.L., Chiang, C.P. & Loef, M. (1989). Using knowledge of children's mathematics thinking in classroom teaching: an experimental study. *American Educational Research Journal*, 26(4): 499–531.

Carter, D., Frobisher, L. & Roper, T. (1994). Assessing mathematical achievement. In A. Orton & G. Wain (eds), *Issues in teaching mathematics* (pp. 117–35). London: Cassell.

Case, R. (1991). A developmental approach to the design of remedial instruction. In A. McKeough & J. Lupart (eds), *Toward the practice of theory-based instruction* (pp. 117–47). Hillsdale, NJ: Erlbaum.

Chen, C., Lee, S.Y. & Stevenson, H.W. (1993). Students' achievement and mathematics instruction: Chinese and Japanese classrooms. In G. Bell (ed.), *Asian perspectives on mathematics education* (pp. 21–35). Lismore, NSW: Northern Rivers Mathematical Association.

Chinn, S.J. & Ashcroft, J.R. (1998). *Mathematics for dyslexics: a teaching handbook* (2nd edn). London: Whurr.

Choate, J.S. (ed.) (1997). *Successful inclusive teaching* (2nd edn). Boston: Allyn & Bacon.

Clark, M. (1999). Calculators as learning tools in mathematics lessons. *Equals: Mathematics and Special Educational Needs*, 5(1): 11–14.

Clayton, P. (1999). It all adds up. *Special Children*, 122: 30–2.

Clemson, D. & Clemson, W. (1994). *Mathematics in the early years*. London: Routledge.

Clopton, E.L. (1992). Ask questions that build confidence. *Mathematics Teacher*, 85: 30.

Cockburn, A.D. (1999). *Teaching mathematics with insight*. London: Falmer.

Coffland, J.A. & Cuevas, G.J. (1992). *Primary problem-solving in math*. Glenview, Ill.: Good Year Books/Scott Foresman.

Cole, P. & Chan, L. (1990). *Methods and strategies for special education*. New York: Prentice Hall.

Collis, K.F. & Romberg, T.A. (1992). *Collis-Romberg mathematical profiles*. Melbourne: Australian Council for Educational Research.

Conway, R. (1996). Curriculum adaptations. In P. Foreman (ed.), *Integration and inclusion in action* (pp. 145–90). Sydney: Harcourt Brace.

Costello, G.P., Horne, M. & Munro, J. (1992). *Sharing maths learning with children*. Melbourne: Australian Council for Educational Research.

Costello, J. (1991). *Teaching and learning mathematics 11–16*. London: Routledge.

Curriculum Corporation (1999). *Numeracy benchmarks*. Melbourne: Curriculum Corporation.

Daly, T. & Buruma, J. (1997). *Mathematics today: transition*. Sydney: McGraw Hill.

Dawe, L. (1993). Visual imagery and communication in the mathematics classroom. In M. Stephens, A. Waywood, D. Clarke & J. Izard (eds), *Communicating mathematics* (pp. 60–76). Melbourne: Australian Council for Educational Research.

Demetriou, A., Shayer, M. & Efklides, A. (1992). *Neo-Piagetian theories of cognitive development*. London: Routledge.

Department of Education and Science (1982). *Mathematics counts: the Cockcroft report*. London: HMSO.

Dick, W. (1992). An instructional designer's view of constructivism. In T.M. Duffy & D. Jonassen (eds), *Constructivism and technology of instruction* (pp. 91–8). Hillsdale, NJ: Erlbaum.

Dienes, Z. (1963). *An experimental study of mathematics learning*. London: Hutchinson.

Dienes, Z. (1964). *The power of mathematics*. London: Hutchinson.

Dienes, Z. (1973). *The six stages in the process of learning mathematics*. Windsor: NFER Publishing.

Doig, B. (1991). *Diagnostic mathematics profiles (DIAMAP)*. Melbourne: Australian Council for Educational Research.

Doig, B. & Lokan, J. (1997). *Learning from children: mathematics from a classroom perspective*. Melbourne: Australian Council for Educational Research.

Drosdeck, C. (1995). Promoting calculator use in the elementary classroom. *Teaching Children Mathematics*, 1(5): 300–5.

Ellison, C. (1998). The national literacy and numeracy strategies: the Commonwealth perspective. *Unicorn*, 24(2): 18–31.

Enright, B.E. & Choate, J.S. (1997). Mathematical problem-solving: the goal of mathematics. In J.S. Choate (ed.), *Successful inclusive teaching* (2nd edn) (pp. 280–303). Boston: Allyn & Bacon.

Farrell, P., Critchley, C. & Mills, C. (1999). The educational attainment of pupils with emotional and behavioural difficulties. *British Journal of Special Education*, 26(1): 50–3.

Fletcher, H. (1970). *Mathematics for schools: teacher's resource book*. London: Addison-Wesley.

Flood, A. (1999). What mental strategies do children use to develop understanding of number? *Equals: Mathematics and Special Educational Needs*, 5(1): 6–8.

Foster, R. (1998). Haven't we found out all we can about children's early number? *Mathematics in School*, 27(3): 2–6.

Frobisher, L. (1994). Problems, investigations and an investigative approach. In A. Orton & G. Wain (eds), *Issues in teaching mathematics* (pp. 150–73). London: Cassell.

Fuchs, L.S. & Fuchs, D. (1998). General educators' instructional adaptation for students with learning disabilities. *Learning Disabilities Quarterly*, 21: 23–33.

Gagne, E.D., Yekovich, C.W. & Yekovich, F.R. (1993). *The cognitive psychology of school learning* (2nd edn). New York: Harper Collins.

Galton, M., Hargreaves, L., Comber, C., Wall, D. & Pell, A. (1999). *Inside the primary classroom: 20 years on*. London: Routledge.

Gersten, R. & Chard, D. (1999). Number sense: rethinking arithmetic instruction for students with mathematical disabilities. *Journal of Special Education*, 33(1): 18–28.

Ginsburg, H. (1989). *Children's arithmetic: how they learn it and how you teach it*. Austin: ProEd.

Good, T., Mulryan, C. & McCaslin, M. (1992). Group instruction in mathematics. In D.A. Grouws (ed.), *Handbook of research on mathematics teaching and learning* (pp. 165–96). New York: Macmillan.

Gooding, A. & Stacey, K. (1993). How children help each other learn in groups. In M. Stephens, A. Waywood, D. Clarke & J. Izard (eds), *Communicating mathematics* (pp. 41–50). Melbourne: Australian Council for Educational Research.

Goulding, M. (1997). *Learning to teach mathematics*. London: Fulton.

Graham, S. & Harris, K.R. (1994). Implications of constructivism for teaching reading and writing to students with special needs. *Journal of Special Education*, 28(3): 275–89.

Grant, S.G. (1998). *Reforming reading, writing and mathematics*. Mahwah, NJ: Erlbaum.

Grauberg, E. (1998). *Elementary mathematics and language difficulties*. London: Whurr.

Greene, G. (1999). Mnemonic multiplication fact instruction for students with learning disabilities. *Learning Disabilities: Research and Practice*, 14(3): 141–8.

Greenes, C., Schulman, L. & Spungin, R. (1992). Stimulating communication in mathematics. *Arithmetic Teacher*, 40(2): 78–82.

Griffin, S.A., Case, R. & Siegler, R.S. (1994). 'Rightstart': providing the central conceptual prerequisites for first formal learning of arithmetic to students at risk for school failure. In K. McGilly (ed.), *Classroom lessons: integrating cognitive theory and classroom practise* (pp. 25–49). Cambridge: MIT Press.

Harris, A. (1999). *Teaching and learning in the effective school*. Aldershot: Ashgate.

Hastings, N. & Schwiesco, J. (1995). Tasks and tables: the effects of seating arrangements in primary classrooms. *Educational Research*, 37(3): 279–91.

Hawthorne, W. (1992). *Young children and mathematics*. Canberra: Australian Early Childhood Education Association.

Heddens, J.W. & Speer, W.R. (1995). *Today's mathematics: concepts and classroom methods* (8th edn). Englewood Cliffs, NJ: Prentice Hall.

Hembree, R. & Marsh, H. (1993). Problem-solving in early childhood: building foundations. In R.J. Jensen (ed.), *Research ideas for the classroom: early childhood mathematics* (pp. 151–70). New York: Macmillan.

Herman, S.J. (1994). Connecting math performance to the representation of mathematical ideas: a study of 6th grade students in China, Japan, Taiwan and the USA. PhD dissertation. Santa Barbara: University of California.

Herr, T. & Johnson, K. (1994). *Problem-solving strategies: crossing the river with dogs*. Berkeley: Key Curriculum Press.

Hoover, J.J. & Patton, J.R. (1997*). Curriculum adaptations for students with learning and behaviour problems* (2nd edn). Austin: ProEd.

Hopkins, S. (1998). Learning-disabled (LD) performance under pressure. In D. Greaves & P. Jeffery (eds), *Strategies for intervention with special needs students* (pp. 43–61). Melbourne: AREA Press.

Howell, K., Fox, S. & Morehead, M. (1993). *Curriculum-based evaluation* (2nd edn). Pacific Grove: Brooks-Cole.

Hughes, M. (1986). *Children and number*. Oxford: Blackwell.

Hunter, M. (1994). *Enhancing teaching*. New York: Macmillan.

Inagaki, K., Hatano, G. & Morita, E. (1998). Construction of mathematical knowledge through whole-class discussion. *Learning and Instruction*, 8(6): 503–26.

Isaacs, A. & Carroll, W. (1999). Strategies for basic facts instruction. *Teaching Children Mathematics*, 5(9): 508–15.

James, A. (1995). Teaching methods and assessment. In D. Broomes, G. Cumberbatch, A. James & O. Petty (eds), *Teaching primary school mathematics* (pp. 1–28). Kingston: Ian Randle Publishers for UNESCO.

James, F. & Brown, K. (1998). *Effective differentiation*. London: Collins.

Johnson, N. (1999). Coventry numeracy project: mathematics in special school. *Equals: Mathematics and Special Educational Needs*, 4(1): 9–16.

Kamii, C. (1994). *Young children continue to reinvent arithmetic: implications of Piaget's theory.* New York: Teachers College Press.

Kauchak, D.P. & Eggen, P.D. (1998). *Learning and teaching: research-based methods* (3rd edn). Boston: Allyn & Bacon.

Kelly, J.A. (1999). Improving problem-solving through drawings. *Teaching Children Mathematics*, 6(1): 48–51.

Kennedy, L.M. & Tipps, S. (1994). *Guiding children's learning of mathematics* (7th edn). Belmont: Wadsworth.

Killen, R. (1996). *Effective teaching strategies: lessons from research and practice.* Wentworth Falls, NSW: Social Science Press.

Knight, G., Arnold, G., Kelly, S. & Thornley, G. (1995). The mathematical needs of school leavers. In *The best of SET: mathematics.* Melbourne: Australian Council for Educational Research.

Kouba, V.L. & Franklin, K. (1993). Multiplication and division: sense making and meaning. In R.J. Jensen (ed.), *Research ideas for the classroom: early childhood mathematics* (pp. 103–26). New York: Macmillan.

Krulik, S. & Rudnick, J.A. (1995). *The new sourcebook for teaching reasoning and problem-solving in elementary school.* Boston: Allyn & Bacon.

Lee, C. & Lawson, C. (1996). Numeracy through literacy. *Educational Action Research*, 4(1): 59–66.

LeGere, A. (1991). Collaborating and writing in mathematics classrooms. *Mathematics Teacher*, 84(3): 166–71.

LeTendre, G. & Shimizu, H. (1999). Towards a healing society: perspectives from Japanese special education. In H. Daniels & P. Garner (eds), *Inclusive education* (pp. 115–29). London: Kogan Page.

Leutzinger, L.P. (1999). Developing thinking strategies for addition facts. *Teaching Children Mathematics*, 6(1): 14–18.

Liebeck, P. (1984). *How children learn mathematics.* Harmondsworth: Penguin.

Lilburn, P. & Rawson, P. (1993). *Talking maths: encouraging children to explore ideas.* Melbourne: Oxford University Press.

Lipsky, D. & Gartner, A. (1998). Taking inclusion into the future. *Educational Leadership*, 56(2): 78–81.

Lloyd, J.W. & Keller, C.E. (1989). Effective mathematics instruction: development, instruction and program. *Focus on Exceptional Children*, 21(7): 1–10.

Lochhead, J. (1991). Making math mean. In E. von Glaserfeld (ed.), *Radical constructivism in mathematics education* (pp. 75–87). Dordrecht: Kluwer.

Lokan, J., Ford, P. & Greenwood, L. (1996). *Mathematics and science on the line: Australian junior secondary students' performance in TIMSS.* Melbourne: Australian Council for Educational Research.

Lokan, J., Ford, P. & Greenwood, L. (1997). *Mathematics and science on the line: Australian middle primary students' performance in TIMSS.* Melbourne: Australian Council for Educational Research.

Lovell, K. (1978). *The growth of basic mathematics and scientific concepts in children* (6th edn). London: University of London Press.

Lyle, S. (1996). An analysis of collaborative group work in the primary school and factors related to its success. *Language and Education*, 10(1): 13–31.

Ma, L. (1999). *Knowing and teaching elementary mathematics*. Mahwah, NJ: Erlbaum.

Manouchehri, A. & Goodman, T. (1998). Mathematics curriculum reform and teachers: understanding the connections. *Journal of Educational Research*, 92(1): 27–41.

Marsh, L. & Cooke, N. (1996). The effects of using manipulatives in teaching math problem-solving to students with learning disabilities. *Learning Disabilities: Research and Practice*, 11(1): 58–65.

Marsh, M. (1999). Flexible setting: a possible way forward? *Equals: Mathematics and Special Educational Needs*, 5(2): 3–4.

Mastropieri, M., Scruggs, T. & Butcher, K. (1997). How effective is inquiry learning for students with mild disabilities? *Journal of Special Education*, 31(2): 199–211.

McCoy, K. (1995). *Teaching special learners in the general education classroom* (2nd edn). Denver: Love.

McInerney, D.M. & McInerney, V. (1998). *Educational psychology: constructing learning* (2nd edn). Sydney: Prentice Hall.

McIntosh, M.E. (1997). Guide students to better comprehension of word problems. *The Clearing House*, 71(1): 26–32.

Meadows, S. (1993). *The child as thinker*. London: Routledge.

Meadows, S. & Cashdan, A. (1988). *Helping children learn: contributions to a cognitive curriculum*. London: Fulton.

Mevarech, Z.R. (1999). Effects of metacognitive training embedded in cooperative settings on mathematical problem-solving. *Journal of Educational Research*, 92(4): 195–205.

Miles, T.R. & Miles, E. (1992). *Dyslexia and mathematics*. London: Routledge.

Miller, S.P. & Mercer, C.D. (1993). Mnemonics: enhancing the math performance of students with learning difficulties. *Intervention in School and Clinic*, 29: 7–82.

Morgan, C. (1998). *Writing mathematically: the discourse of investigation*. London: Falmer.

Mulligan, J. & Mitchelmore, M. (eds) (1996). *Children's number learning*. Adelaide: Australian Association of Mathematics Teachers.

Mullis, I.V., Martin, M.O., Beaton, A.E., Gonzalez, E., Kelly, D.L. & Smith, T.A. (1997). *Mathematics achievement in the primary years: IEA's Third International Mathematics and Science Study (TIMSS)*. Chestnut Hill, MA: TIMSS Study Centre, Boston College.

National Council of Teachers of Mathematics (1989). *Curriculum and evaluation standards for school mathematics*. Reston, VA: National Council of Teachers of Mathematics.

Newman, A. (1983). *The Newman language of mathematics kit*. Sydney: Harcourt Brace Jovanovich.

Noddings, N. (1990). Constructivism in mathematics education. In R.B. Davis, C.A. Maher & N. Noddings (eds), *Constructivist views on the teaching and learning of mathematics*. Reston, VA: National Council of Teachers of Mathematics.

Nuthall, G. (1999). Learning how to learn: the evolution of students' minds through the social culture of the classroom. *International Journal of Educational Research*, 31(3): 141–256.

O'Brien, T.C. (1999). Parrot math. *Phi Delta Kappan*, 80(6): 434–8.

Office for Standards in Education (OFSTED) (1993). *The teaching and learning of number in primary schools*. London: HMSO.

Orton, A. (1994a). The aims of teaching mathematics. In A. Orton & G. Wain (eds), *Issues in teaching mathematics* (pp. 1–20). London: Cassell.

Orton, A. (1994b). Learning mathematics: implications for teaching. In A. Orton & G. Wain (eds), *Issues in teaching mathematics* (pp. 35–57). London: Cassell.

Ostoja, N. (1997). Effective teaching strategies for students experiencing learning difficulties in upper primary and secondary school. In D. Greaves & P. Jeffery (eds), *Learning difficulties, disabilities and resource teaching* (pp. 153–8). Melbourne: AREA Press.

Palmer, D., Kays, M., Smith, A. & Doig, B. (1994). *Stop! look and lesson*. Melbourne: Australian Council for Educational Research.

Patton, J., Cronin, M., Bassett, D. & Koppel, A. (1997). A life skills approach to mathematics instruction. *Journal of Learning Disabilities*, 30(2): 178–87.

Payne, J.N. & Huinker, D.M. (1993). Early number and numeration. In R.J. Jensen (ed.), *Research ideas for the classroom: early childhood mathematics* (pp. 43–71). New York: Macmillan.

Payne, T. & Turner, E. (1999). *Dyslexia: a parents' and teachers' guide*. Clevedon: Multilingual Matters.

Peach, F. (1998). The national literacy and numeracy strategies: implications for educators. *Unicorn*, 24(2): 7–17.

Piaget, J. & Szeminska, A. (1952). *The child's conception of number*. London: Routledge.

Ploetzner, R., Dillenbourg, P., Preier, M. & Traum, D. (1999). Learning by explaining to oneself and to others. In Dillenbourg, P. (ed.), *Collaborative learning: cognitive and computational approaches* (pp. 103–21). Amsterdam: Pergamon.

Polya, G. (1957). *How to solve it: a new aspect of mathematical method*. Princeton, NJ: Princeton University Press.

Polya, G. (1962). *Mathematical discovery*. New York: Wiley.

Pound, L. (1999). *Supporting mathematical development in the early years*. Buckingham: Open University Press.

Pressley, M. & McCormick, C.B. (1995). *Advanced educational psychology for educators, researchers and policy-makers*. New York: Harper Collins.

Prichard, M.K. & Bingaman, S. (1993). Instructional activities and decisions. In P.S. Wilson (ed.), *Research ideas for the classroom: high school mathematics* (pp. 217–31). New York: Macmillan.

Recht, E., Forster, M. & Masters, G. (1998). *Developmental assessment resource for teachers: DART Mathematics*. Melbourne: Australian Council for Educational Research.

Reynolds, D. & Farrell, S. (1996). *Worlds apart: a review of international surveys of educational achievement involving England*. London: HMSO.

Reys, R., Suydam, M., Lindquist, M. & Smith, N. (1998). *Helping children learn mathematics* (5th edn). Boston: Allyn & Bacon.

Richards, J. (1996). Negotiating the negotiation of meaning. In L. Steffe & P. Nesher (eds), *Theories of mathematical learning* (pp. 69–75). Mahwah, NJ: Erlbaum.

Robitaille, D.F. (1993). *Curriculum frameworks for mathematics and science*. Vancouver: Pacific Educational Press.

Robitaille, D.F. (ed.) (1997). *National contexts for mathematics and science education*. Vancouver: Pacific Educational Press.

Romberg, T.A. (1993). How one comes to know: models and theories of the learning of mathematics. In M. Niss (ed.), *Investigations into assessment in mathematics education* (pp. 97–111). Dordrecht: Kluwer.

Romberg, T.A. (ed.) (1995). *Reform in school mathematics and authentic assessment*. Albany: University of New York Press.

Rosenshine, B. & Meister, C. (1994). Reciprocal teaching: a review of research. *Review of Educational Research*, 64(4): 479–530.

Rowe, M.B. (1986). Wait time: slowing down may be a way of speeding up. *Journal of Teacher Education*, 37(1): 43–50.

Sabornie, E.J. & deBettencourt, L.U. (1997). *Teaching students with mild disabilities at the secondary level*. Columbus: Merrill.

Salend, S.J. (1994). *Effective mainstreaming* (2nd edn). New York: Macmillan.

Sawada, D. (1999). Mathematics as problem-solving: a Japanese way. *Teaching Children Mathematics*, 6(1): 54–8.

Schaub, M. & Baker, D.P. (1994). What makes for effective mathematics instruction? Japanese and American classrooms compared. In I. Westbury, C.A. Ethington, L. Sosniak & D.P. Baker (eds), *In search of more effective mathematics education* (pp. 151–67). Norwood, NJ: Ablex Publishing.

Scott, B., Vitale, M.R. & Masten, W.G. (1998). Implementing instructional adaptations for students with disabilities in inclusive classrooms. *Remedial and Special Education*, 19(2): 106–19.

Serna, L. & Patton, J. (1997). Mathematics. In E. Polloway & J. Patton (eds), *Strategies for teaching learners with special needs* (6th edn) (pp. 312–62). Columbus: Merrill.

Sheffield, L.J. & Cruikshank, D.E. (1996). *Teaching and learning elementary and middle school mathematics* (3rd edn). Columbus: Merrill.

Shimizu, Y. (1995). Some pluses and minuses of typical form in mathematics lessons: a Japanese perspective. In G. Bell (ed.), *Review of mathematics education in Asia and the Pacific*. Lismore, NSW: Southern Cross Mathematical Association.

Silver, E.A. (1997). Learning from NAEP: looking back and looking ahead. In P. Kenney & E.A. Silver (eds), *Results from the Sixth Mathematics Assessment of the National Assessment of Educational Progress* (pp. 279–87). Reston, VA: National Council of Teachers of Mathematics.

Simmons, M. (1993). *The effective teaching of mathematics*. London: Longman.

Simon, M.A. (1997). Developing new models of mathematics teaching: an imperative for research on mathematics teacher development. In E. Fennema & B.S. Nelson (eds), *Mathematics teachers in transition* (pp. 55–86). Mahwah, NJ: Erlbaum.

Skemp. R. (1989a). *Mathematics in the primary school*. London: Routledge.

Skemp. R. (1989b). *Structured activities for primary mathematics*. London: Routledge.

Sophian, C. (1996). *Children's number*. Boulder, Colorado: Westview Press.

Sotto, E. (1994). *When teaching becomes learning*. London: Cassell.

Souviney, R.J. (1994). *Learning to teach mathematics* (2nd edn). New York: Macmillan.

Sowder, J., Philipp, R., Armstrong, B. & Schappelle, B. (1998). *Middle-grade teachers' mathematical knowledge and its relationship to instruction*. Albany: University of New York Press.

Stacey, K. (1997). Classroom views of problem-solving in context. In B. Doig & J. Lokan (eds), *Learning from children: mathematics from a classroom perspective* (pp. 63–76). Melbourne: Australian Council for Educational Research.

Stading, M., Williams, R. & McLaughlin, T.F. (1996). Effects of cover, copy and compare procedure on multiplication facts mastery with a third-grade girl with learning disabilities in a home setting. *Education and Treatment of Children*, 19(4): 425–34.

Staves, L. (1999a). Making it count. *Special Children*, 120: 23–6.

Staves, L. (1999b). Counter intelligence. *Special Children*, 121: 25–7.

Steen, L.A. (1997). The new literacy. In L.A. Steen (ed.), *Why numbers count* (pp. xv–xxviii). New York: College Entrance Examination Board.

Steen, L.A. (1999). Twenty questions about mathematical reasoning. In L.V. Stiff & F.R. Curcio (eds), *Developing mathematical reasoning in grades K–12* (pp. 270–85). Reston, VA: National Council of Teachers of Mathematics.

Stenmark, J.K. (1991). *Mathematics assessment: myths, models, good questions and practical suggestions*. Reston, VA: National Council of Teachers of Mathematics.

Sternberg, R.J. (1999). The nature of mathematical reasoning. In L.V. Stiff & F.R. Curcio (eds), *Developing mathematical reasoning in grades K–12* (pp. 37–44). Reston, VA: National Council of Teachers of Mathematics.

Stevenson, H., Lummis, M., Lee, S.Y. & Stigler, J. (1990). *Making the grade in mathematics*. Reston, VA: National Council of Teachers of Mathematics.

Stevenson, H.W. & Stigler, J.W. (1992). *The learning gap*. New York: Simon & Schuster.

Stewart, W. (1997). Issues in teaching mathematics to students with specific learning disability. In P. Westwood & W. Stewart, *Basic mathematics for students with learning difficulties* (pp. 43–57). Adelaide: Institute for the Study of Learning Difficulties.

Stigler, J.W., Fernandez, C. & Yoshida, M. (1996). Traditions of school mathematics in Japanese and American classrooms. In L. Steffe & P. Nesher (eds), *Theories of mathematical learning* (pp. 149–75). Mahwah, NJ: Erlbaum.

Stigler, J.W. & Hiebert, J. (1997). Understanding and improving classroom mathematics instruction. *Phi Delta Kappan*, 79(1): 14–21.

Stigler, J.W. & Hiebert, J. (1999). *The teaching gap*. New York: Free Press.

Stoessiger, R. & Wilkinson, M. (1991). Emergent mathematics. *Education*, 3(13): 3–11.

Swanson, H.L. (1999). *Interventions for students with learning disabilities: a meta-analysis of treatment outcomes*. New York: Guilford.

Tarver, S. (1996). Direct instruction. In W. Stainback & S. Stainback (eds), *Controversial issues confronting special education* (2nd edn) (pp. 143–52). Boston: Houghton Mifflin.

Thelfall, J. (1996). The role of practical apparatus in the teaching and learning of mathematics. *Educational Review*, 48(1): 3–12.

Tomlinson, C. (1995). *How to differentiate instruction in mixed-ability classrooms*. Alexandria: Association for Supervision and Curriculum Development.

Tuovinen, J.E. & Sweller, J. (1999). A comparison of cognitive load associated with discovery learning and worked examples. *Journal of Educational Psychology*, 91(2): 334–41.

Usnick, V. & McCoy, K.M. (1995). Mathematics instruction. In K.M. McCoy (ed.), *Teaching special learners in the general education classroom* (2nd edn) (pp. 395–440). Denver: Love.

Van de Walle, J.A. (1998). *Elementary and middle school mathematics: teaching developmentally* (3rd edn). New York: Longman.

Van den Heuvel-Panhuizen, M. (1996). *Assessment and realistic mathematics education*. Utrecht: Freudenthal Institute.

Van Oers, B. (1996). Learning mathematics as meaningful activity. In L. Steffe, P. Nesher, P. Cobb, G. Goldin & B. Greer (eds), *Theories of mathematical learning* (pp. 91–113). Mahwah, NJ: Erlbaum.

Vaughn, S., Bos, C. & Schumm, J. (1997). *Teaching mainstreamed, diverse, and at-risk students in the general education classroom*. Boston: Allyn & Bacon.

Vygotsky, L. (1962). *Thought and language*. Cambridge: MIT Press.

Wain, G. (1994). Mathematics education and society. In A. Orton & G. Wain (eds), *Issues in teaching mathematics* (pp. 21–34). London: Cassell.

Wakefield, A.P. (1997). Supporting math thinking. *Phi Delta Kappan*, 79(3): 233–6.

Waters, M. & Montgomery, P. (1993). Mathematics: multiplying the learning. In M. Stephens, A. Waywood, D. Clarke & J. Izard (eds), *Communicating mathematics* (pp. 191–208). Melbourne: Australian Council for Educational Research.

Watson, A. (1999). Paradigmatic conflicts in informal mathematics assessment as sources of social inequity. *Educational Review*, 51(2): 105–15.

Watson, J. (1999). Working in groups: social and cognitive effects in a special class. *British Journal of Special Education*, 26(2): 87–95.

Westwood, P.S. (1997). *Commonsense methods for children with special needs* (3rd edn). London: Routledge.

Westwood, P.S. (1998). Which intervention? Effective strategies to overcome learning difficulties. In D. Greaves & P. Jeffery (eds), *Strategies for intervention with special needs students* (pp. 177–99). Melbourne: AREA Press.

Westwood, P.S. (1999). Constructivist approaches to mathematics learning: a note of caution. In D. Barwood, D. Greaves & P. Jeffery (eds), *Teaching numeracy and literacy: interventions and strategies for 'at-risk' students* (pp. 175–89). Melbourne: AREA Press.

Whitebread, D. (1995). Emergent mathematics or how to help young children become confident mathematicians. In J. Anghileri (ed.), *Children's mathematical thinking in the primary years* (pp. 11–40). London: Cassell.

Wiliam, D., Boaler, J. & Brown, M. (1999). 'We've still got to learn': low-attainers' experiences of setting. *Equals: Mathematics and Special Educational Needs*, 5(1): 15–18.

Willis, S. (1998). Which numeracy? *Unicorn*, 24(2): 32–42.

Wilson, J.W., Fernandez, M.L. & Hadaway, N. (1993). Mathematical problem-solving. In P. Wilson (ed.), *Research ideas for the classroom: high school mathematics* (pp. 57–78). New York: Macmillan.

Wong, N.Y. (1993). Mathematics education in Hong Kong: developments in the last decade. In G. Bell (ed.), *Asian perspectives on mathematics education* (pp. 56–69). Lismore, NSW: Northern Rivers Mathematical Association.

Wood, D. (1998). *How children think and learn* (2nd edn). Oxford: Blackwell.

Xin, Y.P. & Jitendra, A.K. (1999). The effects of instruction in solving mathematical word problems for students with learning problems: a meta-analysis. *Journal of Special Education*, 32(4): 207–25.

Zepp, R. (1989). *Language and mathematics education*. Hong Kong: API Press.

Index

individualised work 13, 33, 34, 40
instrumental understanding 26, 53, 66
intellectual disability 18, 24, 28, 103, 104
interactive whole-class teaching 34, 40
international studies of math attainment 10
interventions for learning difficulties 68, 74, 75, 81, 83
interviewing for assessment purposes 79–80, 81, 83, 98, 99
inventory of basic skills 78, 83–84

J

Japanese teaching methods 11–13
journals: for mathematics teaching 101

K

Keymath: assessment kit 98–99
kindergarten: learning in 17, 21, 22, 29, 47, 63

L

language:
    importance in learning mathematics 6, 11, 18, 26, 38, 48, 56, 95
    teacher's use of 19, 35
    role in diagnosis 19, 32
learned helplessness 2
learning:
    in the early years 3–4, 17–23, 28, 31, 44, 47, 97
    matching teaching to learning 8, 10, 31, 38
    types of 8–10, 22, 23, 24–25, 31, 38
learning difficulties
    needs of students with 8, 27, 36, 37, 41, 46, 47, 53, 55, 63, 66, 68, 81, 103–104
    possible causes 3–4, 18, 23, 25, 31, 35, 45, 48, 53, 54, 66, 72
learning styles 3, 97
locus of control 2
logico-mathematical knowledge 28
lower-order questioning 36
lower-order skills 9
lower-order thinking 9

M

MAB (multi-base arithmetic blocks) 21, 41, 52, 54, 57, 95
manipulatives
    (*see also* structural apparatus) 41–42, 53, 69, 74
Mathematics Curriculum Profile for Australian Schools 77, 83, 85, 89–90, 99
math phobia 1
memory 45
    long-term 3, 10, 46
    short-term 45, 46
    working memory 45, 70, 96
    emorisation 10, 32, 46–47, 57, 59, 63
mental computation 9, 33, 42, 45, 47, 60, 84, 89
metacognition: in mathematics learning and problem solving 8, 22, 65, 67, 74
'min' strategy for counting 44, 45, 84
mixed-ability teaching
    (*see also* differentiation) 36, 39
mnemonics: as an aid to recall 47, 73
money skills and concepts 85, 87, 88, 103, 104
monitoring:
    as a function of teaching 33, 40
    self-monitoring 8, 65, 67, 68, 79
Mortensen mathematics equipment 21
multiple embodiment 59
multiplication 55–58, 86, 88
    algorithms in 58–59
    teaching of 56–58

N

National statement on mathematics for Australian schools 2, 43, 64, 104
neo-Piagetian perspectives on learning 22
non-routine problems 64–65, 69
number facts 5, 33, 45, 66, 80, 82, 86, 88, 104
    automaticity in 9, 45, 80, 104
    how to improve 74, 97, 99
    importance of 33, 45
number line: as teaching aid 50, 80
number recognition 28, 43, 84
number sentences 49, 50, 56, 69, 85
number skills: teaching of 43–61

student-centred learning 5, 7, 31, 32, 34

subtraction 4, 52
    algorithms 54–55
    decomposition method 51, 54
    teaching of 47, 50, 54–55

symbolic representation 21, 25, 47, 48

symbolic stage of development 21, 25, 55

T

tally marks: as a bridge for recording 47, 50, 80, 92

teacher education: in mathematics 5

teachers' role as facilitators 6, 7, 26, 35, 68

teacher as instructor 4, 7, 35, 68

teacher-made tests 78, 84, 90–91

teaching methods 3, 6, 11, 12–14, 31, 32–36, 43–45, 53–60, 67

testing 34, 98
    how much is needed? 34, 91
    in program planning 77–78
    types of 77, 90–92, 97–100

thematic studies 33–34

thinking aloud: as a teaching strategy 19, 67, 68

time-telling: as a component of the curriculum 85, 105

time: as an issue in lesson planning and teaching 53

TIMSS (Third International Mathematics and Science Study) 1, 7, 12, 33, 39

transmission model of teaching 4, 35

U

United States: teaching approaches and standards 10, 12, 13

Unifix 21, 41, 50, 59, 71

V

verbal cueing 54–55

visual aids: role of 40, 41, 70

visual approaches to learning and teaching 21, 35, 40, 46–47, 50, 51, 59, 70

visual imagery 41, 46, 50, 52, 56, 70

visualisation: as a teaching technique 56, 65, 70, 73, 74

vocabulary
    assessment of 80, 84
    importance in learning 18, 48, 74, 80
    importance in teaching 40, 48, 74

Vygotsky, L. 18, 22, 25–26, 32

W

wait time: in questioning 36

whole-class teaching 12,. 13, 33, 34

word problems 64

work samples 78, 81–82, 90, 98

working memory 70, 96

writing in mathematics 20, 81

Z

zone of proximal development 25–26, 32, 92